Endorsements

Life can be a struggle. At times, we get bruised and battered. When I first got to know Grace, she was suffering an ongoing physical ordeal, on top of the effects of bullying behaviour by an employer, rejection by a close friend and the daily challenges of accepting personal care carried out by strangers. Through it all, Grace maintained a trust in Jesus. This is a truly inspiring account of the unique and personal way in which He demonstrated He is worthy of such trust. I witnessed at first hand Grace's remarkable healing. Yet, time and again, this story points to God's precious and powerful presence in the long journey of suffering.

Revd John Western – Minister of Westcliff Baptist Church

I have seen Grace in her wheelchair, very frail and very fragile, and I have seen Grace walking tall, all shining with health. In both conditions, her faith in holding tight to the Lord was obvious. This is a remarkable story of miraculous divine healing, but it is the even more remarkable story of Grace's journey into allowing healing into all her hurt places!

Jennifer Rees Larcombe
Founder of Beauty From Ashes Trust
Author of: Journey Into God's Heart
Publisher: Hodder & Stoughton

RELEASED TO
ROAR

RELEASED TO
ROAR

Moving From TRAPPED In PAIN
To TRUSTING In PROMISES
And Becoming TRIUMPHANT In PURPOSE

GRACE HABBERSHAW

⌐AUTHOR ⪥
ACADEMY elite

Published by Author Academy Elite
P.O. Box 43, Powell, OH 43035
AuthorAcademyElite.com

Cover Design by Robert Roth

Printed in the United States of America

DISCLAIMER:
The stories in this book have been recreated from the best of my memory. Names have been changed to respect the privacy of the individuals involved. I write that the glory will go to God the Father, Jesus His Son, and the power of the Holy Spirit, to be witnessed by every reader.

All Scripture quotations, unless otherwise marked, are taken from The Holy Bible, New International Version®

Copyright © 1973, 1978, 1984, by International Bible Society.

ISBN-Paperback: 978-1-946114-94-5
ISBN-Hardback: 978-1-64085-026-2

Library of Congress Control Number: 2017909082
Author Academy Elite, Powell, OH

Dedication

To Jesus, the author and perfecter of my faith, my Rock, without Him, my life is nothing.

To my children and grandchildren, I am rich beyond compare! I love you - beyond words; and I am so proud of you all - beyond measure! Thank you for loving me, in and through all things.

To my siblings, thank you for your love and support. Separated by the miles but always joined at the heart.

To my God Given Best Friend, through whom I have learned so much! Thank you for your courage, your grace, your sacrifice, and your servant heart. Tears were endured for a night, but joy came in the morning!

But he knows the way that I take;
when he has tested me, I shall come forth as gold.
Job 23:10

To everyone who surrounded me with love, compassion, encouragement, and a servant heart in and through all things. You were the 'love, the 'hand', the 'ears', the 'heart', the 'eyes', the 'voice', and the 'embrace' of Jesus into my life in every situation. I would not be who I am today without you! You are all unique, all precious, so loved, and never forgotten. You know who you are!

Contents

Foreword

In the beginning, there is God. At the end there is God. But how do we navigate that 'wobbly' bit in the middle, called 'Life'?

Life is a progressive drama where choices and consequences shape us into who we ultimately become. Hope often fades when the circumstances of our life are not what we expected them to be.

But, if we choose to capture our thoughts, confront in truth, choose our responses, and communicate in love, nothing is impossible!

We focus on the destination—what we would like to happen—but the journey we take is just as important.

Our author began as a sickly, stammering child raised in a large family. She had no sense of confidence or identity, and so she hid behind the uniform as a police officer. She went through marriage, motherhood, divorce, and the near loss of her children through accidents and illness. She stumbled through severed friendships and shattered dreams. Life was a roller coaster of emotions and brokenness.

But Grace is far from being a 'victim'!

Nothing remains the same forever, but how we think of the situations and changing episodes of life and the choices that we make, all determine how we journey through it. Everybody is different, and so are our situations.

We can have a different outcome to everyone else because we make wiser, healthier choices, and we set ourselves up for victory, because we 'did' something different to 'have' something different.

This was Grace's experience. She had to make significant choices as she encountered twelve years of debilitating chronic sickness, becoming wheelchair dependent for seven years, and losing her audible voice. These conditions threw her into momentary depths of despair and nearly took her life.

Stripped of everything and, in control of nothing, her faith raised her up to new heights. In spite of everything, she emerged triumphant.

Her belief was challenged to the max as she held onto God's promises. Her victory would not only liberate her into physical freedom, but also into her true identity. She finally understood the call over her life, to serve and minister in all the fullness of His grace.

But, to achieve all that, she had to 'go through' to 'come through.' You do too.

It is so easy to want our trials to come to an end quickly, for everything to be as we would like it to be. But, there are riches to be claimed beyond compare, when we endure with courage.

It takes grace to accept help when you prefer to give; to focus not on what has been lost, but on what has been gained. It takes patience; to choose to look beyond ourselves and our situations, and see other people in their moment of need too. We must adjust if we want to consider all perspectives and not just our own and to choose to give, not just take. In every negative situation, there is positivity to be found too, if we choose to see it!

As Grace shares her journey of struggle, loss and suffering through twelve years of emotional and debilitating physical pain, her heart is for you to be inspired. She hopes you will experience transparency of heart, love for others, grace in abandonment, breaking negative prognosis, standing on the promises of God, experiencing faith, have hope in vision, honour in humour, and to witness the freedom and joy of her ultimate healing that changed everyone's perspective of how to endure adversity.

Grace has found her true voice, to ROAR in power and impact, to touch a hurting world for Jesus.

Be encouraged to believe for the best, no matter what life holds.

If you don't like your life, it's time to start changing your choices!

Kary Oberbrunner-Author of *ELIXIR Project,*
Day Job to Dream Job, The Deeper Path and Your
Secret Name

Introduction

If you are holding this book in your hand, then today, you are alive and breathing. If you have opened this book in the morning – what does your day hold for you? You may have plans to relax with family or friends, or you may have to go to work or be facing a health crisis, or have worries beyond measure.

If you are holding this book in the evening – what has your day been like? How many of the intentions that you considered this morning, as you woke up, have you achieved? How much has life cut across your plans, and your day has not been as you expected it to be?

Whatever your answers to these questions, I can guarantee one thing: today, your life has been impacted by choices!

Not only by choices that you have made for yourself, both good and bad – but also by choices made for you by other people.

Choices and consequences shape us to be who we are, as we journey through the different dramas and traumas of life. So often, we lose hope as things do not turn out in the way that we expect.

If only we would 'hold our thoughts' before responding or reacting; then choose to 'confront truth' rather than live in denial, and be able to 'communicate in love' instead of in pain and anger – then nothing would be impossible.

We focus on the destination ...what we would *like* to happen...but the journey that we take is just as important!

This is my story of *'one moment in time'* that changed my life forever! - A journey of struggle, loss and suffering, through twelve years of emotional, and debilitating physical pain - as a consequence of a simple road accident that was 'someone else's' fault.

But, I had been in this place many times before. Born into a large family, and constantly missing school due to sickness, I was bullied as a child because I stammered. Lacking in confidence and not sure of my identity, I became a police officer, able to hide behind the authority of the uniform. Marriage, motherhood, divorce, the near loss of my children through sickness and accidents, broken friendships and shattered dreams, all took their toll and fractured my identity. I was affected by other people's choices!

However, they also took me through a journey of 'searching' and exposure of who I really am, and helped to prepare me for what was to come.

By writing this book I have taken ownership of my story; to confront in truth the negatives, the positives and the messiness of life in all its fullness, as this particular part of my life journey unfolded.

It is a journey from:

PAIN to PEACE, GUILT to GRACE, FEAR to FAITH, HURT to HOPE and from CONFUSION to CLARITY.

I became a believer in Jesus, who is the Son of God, in 1985, but I know and understand, that not everybody who chooses to read this book will perhaps believe the same as I do. But that is okay. Again, it is about our *'free will choice,'* and I honour you in what you choose to believe. Therefore, this is a book for everybody to read, no matter where your heart stands.

However, I cannot deny the impact that God has had on my life, in and through all things. Therefore, He is woven into my natural expression of truths as they were encountered. And if it wasn't for His power at work in my life, I would not have a story to tell!

God 'speaks' to me in many ways. I do not hear an audible voice, but He knows how to get my attention. Sometimes it is through reading the Bible, or through watching/listening to Christian teaching, or often through things that other people say. But it is mostly out of the journey that I have taken, to seek His heart and understand His ways.

However He chooses to guide my steps, it is through a deep seated 'knowing' in my heart, and a peace that settles over me, that I just 'know, that I know, that I know', what I should do.

I hope my story will inspire you to:

'*Hope*' for better things to come, whatever your journey so far, to make healthier choices and claim victory in and through all things.

Be '*Encouraged*' to believe for the best no matter what life holds, and choose to receive the help that is available for us all, if we choose to claim it. We are created to be relational, not to live isolated and alone. Many believe it is weak to ask for, or receive, help. But we are all in need of family and friendship, so that we can work together.

'*Endure*' and embrace adversity with courage, to overcome!

All I know is, I have lived a journey of incredible **Pain**, but I have been released in power!

I have seen **Promises** fulfilled and now I walk in freedom!

I understand more of my **Purpose**, and I will live it out for the rest of my life!

So, what choice will you make today?

If you don't like your life, it's time to start changing your choices!

Yeshua's words came back to me:

"There is far more to be revealed in time.
Only then will you be able
to follow where I go."

"And where will you go, Master?
Where will you lead me?"

It was a mystery. I would trust,
absent of that knowledge, for this was faith.

Ted Dekker
(Book A.D.30)

PART ONE

A LIFE CHANGING EXPERIENCE

1

One Moment in Time

In that moment of disorientation the silence is almost deafening, and then, as I re-focus, the sound of the indicator ticking, of music playing on the radio and the inherent stillness of both of our bodies suddenly becomes so real. Then I remember the preceding moment...

I was leaning forward to reach something in the footwell of the car, then suddenly, I am thrown backward, and as my body hits the chair back it collapses and I fall backward again into a reclined position. A searing pain momentarily runs across my lower back and I am immediately concerned about the spinal fusion surgery that I had gone through many years before. As I try to comprehend what has happened the pain subsides very quickly.

Suddenly, I am aware that our car is sitting across the roundabout we had momentarily stopped at, and we are in the path of oncoming traffic. I look to the driver, my best friend Esther, and I am concerned for her well-being. A brief conversation confirms she has no pain, and we both agree that we feel okay.

Though retired from service, my training as a police officer kicked in and I was able to take charge of the situation. The rear end of the car is heavily stove in from the point of impact, but the car is still drivable. The offending vehicle behind us is damaged at the front, but both cars are able to be easily moved to the side of the road to clear the area for other traffic to flow, so that is what we did. Once we were safe in the lay-by we got out of the car to sort legalities with the other driver, a local taxi operator who knew the area well, and who was loudly protesting, "This roundabout is always clear!" As we talked it became apparent that he was speeding and driving on autopilot. The outside lane of the dual carriageway approach to the roundabout had been completely clear, so he could have just driven around us, but he admitted that he had just not seen our car and had driven at the roundabout without slowing down, because "This roundabout is always clear!"

As we exchanged insurance, personal and vehicle details the shock of what he had done suddenly hit him, and the man collapsed in tears and apologies for what he had caused to happen to us. As we stood at the side of the road I put my arms around him and he just sobbed uncontrollably into my shoulder. I reassured him that accidents happen, we were all okay, the cars were damaged but both could easily be repaired, so we all had so much to be thankful for.

All practicalities sorted, he helped us to check that the car was still drivable and we continued on our way. The back end was badly damaged and we knew we would only retrieve our cases through access from the back seat as the boot could not be opened, but that was okay. Neither one of us cried, discussed or even considered returning home. Other than Esther telephoning her husband to let him know what had happened, we both stayed focused on getting to our destination.

It was several months earlier that we had booked into the three-day Joyce Meyer Conference being held in Birmingham, UK. We had been watching Joyce, a Christian author, and speaker, on the God TV channel for many years and her teaching had transformed our lives in so many ways.

However, three weeks before we were due to go I suddenly got 'cold feet' about it and considered cancelling my ticket, but as I prayed God confirmed that I had to go as it was going to be a "life changing experience!" I believed that perhaps Joyce would speak something so profound into my life that it would change me forever, but the accident happened on the way there!

We really enjoyed the conference and many profound truths were taught, but over the next three days, I had progressive pain develop in my neck and upper back. I took pain relief and rested at the hotel between sessions but our 'girly weekend' shopping plans were somewhat thwarted! I hadn't done this sort of weekend before and was quite daunted by it, especially sharing a room because I was such a shy, private person, which is one reason why I so nearly cancelled my ticket. Well, that and guilt as a mother, about taking time out just for me! But as we rested we did a lot of talking, laughing and praying. In the years to come, we would do so much more of this together, but encounter many tears of heartache too.

Other than a slight ache in her neck for a couple of days, Esther had no real ill effects from the accident, for which I was thankful. However, as we drove home at the end of the weekend my body went into total muscle spasm and excruciating pain. I didn't want to make a fuss, but on realising the severity of the discomfort, Esther then insisted on taking me to the local Accident and Emergency department where I was diagnosed with severe whiplash.

The car was taken in for repair the following day and was immediately 'written off' by the insurance company. The repairs were too major to warrant the cost involved! It was then we remembered the protection of God over our lives, as we had driven for nearly 300 miles since the road accident in the damaged car!

BUT, I am also thankful for a conversation with my son, who only days before the accident had talked to me about the importance of adjusting the headrest when getting into any car, to make sure it is aligned right to protect head movement should an accident happen. His job experience had shown how many people lose their lives because of poorly positioned headrests. As I got into the car at the start of this trip, those words of wisdom had resonated through my spirit and I had adjusted the headrest before the journey began. I have no doubt that this conversation helped to save my life!

Remembering that God had already said that going to the conference was going to be a "Life changing experience" I was reminded of these verses in the Bible:-

> For I know the plans I have for you," declares the Lord, "plans to prosper you and not to harm you, plans to give you hope and a future. [12] Then you will call on me and come and pray to me, and I will listen to you. [13] You will seek me and find me when you seek me with all your heart. [14] I will be found by you," declares the Lord, "and will bring you back from captivity...
>
> **Jeremiah 29:11-14**

God does have a plan for all of our lives. It wasn't His plan that we had the road accident, but He knew what the other driver was going to do and how we would be caught in the consequence of his actions. But, God turns all things around for our good, even through difficulties, and despite the physical pain I was excited and upbeat about the future. I knew from experience that I could trust God, but I could never have anticipated what was to come. What I had already learned and understood from past experience, was that my choices would become crucial to how I would claim the best for my life.

But Joseph said to them, "Don't be afraid. Am I in the place of God? [20] You intended to harm me, but God intended it for good to accomplish what is now being done, the saving of many lives.

Genesis 50:19-20

2

Falling in Love

The hospital prescribed strong medication and recommended that I take two weeks away from my full-time job to rest, but it should then be alright for me to continue driving and get on with everyday living. However, I was cautioned that complete recovery could take up to eighteen months.

The pain was debilitating and the side effects of the medication were disorientating to say the least, leaving me drowsy but euphoric - such a strange combination! I could barely hold my head up, so I could do very little else except rest. As I could not physically do anything else, and believeing that it was only for two weeks, which was precious time alone when you are divorced and a full time working mum, I knew I had a choice. I could idle my time watching daytime television or put my time to better use.

I have been a believer and follower of Jesus since 1985 and like most people, the journey has taken many twists and turns and ups and downs in my commitment to it. I have either been in full on surrender, adoration, and trust, or, I would choose to live life my way as I forgot to include Him, and I was journeying in my own strength.

As life's dramas unfolded through many scenarios, including moving across country because of my husband's work that took me away from a large supportive family network, and nearly losing a newborn baby to the whooping cough infection; Or going through major back surgery prior to the breakdown of my marriage that culminated in separation and then divorce; Or dealing with the ensuing consequences in the life of a teenage child surviving a major accident but losing his identity; Through these and many other things, I learned to lean into and depend on Jesus for everything.

But, I am human.

In our humanity we let our emotions and imaginations run riot in all directions. We cannot understand why 'bad things' happen to us, we question everything, we challenge everything, we become consumed with the detail and in doing so, we take ourselves down under the circumstances. We love to apportion blame, make excuses, live in denial, become the 'victim', want sympathy, and we give ourselves permission to have a pity party as we lose our focus on everything else.

However, on this occasion, I chose to listen to Christian teaching tapes and CDs, and watch God TV programmes, to build on what I had experienced at the weekend conference. In doing so I just soaked up new revelation and inspiration through truths in the Bible that inspired and encouraged me in my faith journey with Jesus and to believe for better things to come in my life. I was so physically uncomfortable I couldn't even hold my Bible. It was just too heavy to handle. But as I listened to audio messages and teaching, my spirit came alive and I was built up and encouraged, reminded of basic truths of the Christian faith and I fell in love with Jesus all over again!

At the end of the two weeks, I was still in radical pain and discomfort. I could barely move my neck from left to right and any attempt to put my chin down towards my chest almost caused me to pass out. I saw my doctor who signed me off sick for another month and I was referred for x-rays. The results didn't show anything untoward so I was advised to continue with painkillers and rest. My line manager, Barbara, wasn't impressed with my absence and made her feelings known, but there was nothing I could do about it. My job involved driving to visit elderly and disabled clients in their own home to demonstrate and install emergency call equipment that enabled help to be summoned if they fell over or were taken ill etc. There were copious amounts of paperwork to complete and equipment to be sorted and carried. Physically, I could not contend with any of it. But as Barbara concentrated on the need for the job to be fulfilled, her concern for my welfare went by the wayside.

It wasn't until seven months later that I was able to return to work, so there were numerous painful telephone conversations with Barbara as I repeatedly advised my absence on doctor's orders, and she made her feelings well known to me for how I was letting the team down. It was a difficult time and confusing to me. I had worked for the team in different capacities for ten years and I had always had a good relationship with everybody, including management. I was experienced, I trained newcomers into their job, I was delegated responsibilities above my job title because I was so trusted and I was recognised, and encouraged, as someone who would one day take a leadership role in management. So this distancing, wrong accusation and lack of support were distressing, to say the least. I frequently came off the telephone in tears.

But, I had a choice. I could harbour resentment and let Barbara's attitude affect me and ruin our relationship, or, I could forgive and stop a bitter root judgement taking hold that would destroy me and everything that I stand for. I was really challenged and tested in this after every point of contact with my employers, and as I stayed focused on all I was learning in my faith journey I was being tested time and time again. It wasn't always easy, but, I also knew that I had no choice if I wanted freedom.

Forgiveness is the intentional and voluntary process by which a victim undergoes a change in feelings and attitude regarding an offence, choosing to let go of negative emotions such as vengefulness, with an increased ability to wish the offender well.

"To forgive is to set a prisoner free and discover that the prisoner was you. You will know that forgiveness has begun when you recall those who hurt you and feel the power to wish them well."

LEWIS B. SMEDES

I love this definition and quote about forgiveness. I knew I had to choose to forgive in order to set myself free. It didn't matter what anybody else would say or do to me that might be so wrong and cause great upset, the choice I was to make would give me an element of control over the whole situation or make me a victim.

For if you forgive other people when they sin against you, your heavenly Father will also forgive you. ¹⁵ But if you do not forgive others their sins, your Father will not forgive your sins.

Matthew 6:14-15

It is also a biblical truth. Jesus died on the Cross so that when we do something wrong, as we recognise the error of our ways and say a sincere sorry to God, because of His grace over our lives, He will forgive us. But we are also expected to show that same grace to other people who do or say wrong things to us. If we are not able to forgive them, why should God forgive us?

Many people will argue, "Why should I forgive them?" And I understand where they are coming from. But the truth is, we cannot afford not to. If we choose not to forgive,we remain a prisoner of what they did to us and we empower them and give them control over our lives to constantly cause us pain. Our choice to forgive sets us free!

3

Friendship

Although I was following medical advice, the pain in my back and neck continued to increase and the discomfort caused me to become quite isolated. I only left home for medical appointments, so going to Church and everything else went by the wayside for a while. Although a couple of people helped me to attend the appointments, the majority of people just fell away from relationship with me as they continued in the activities of their own lives, and I had to accept that I could not physically fit into social opportunities and demands at that time.

But Esther came through my door nearly every day. We had been friends for 17 years, Jesus was first and foremost in both of our lives and God had a plan for us to journey together in Him and for Him. Esther was a 'missionary kid' and I had only been a believer for two years when we first met, and over the years God has, unknowingly to Esther, mentored me through her life into new understanding in Him.

Our families were very close because our children, her four boys and my two boys and a girl, had grown up together. In fact, Esther became known as "second mum" to my three children as she supported them so many times through family difficulties and traumas, not least when I was hospitalised because of a back injury, that would lead to spinal fusion surgery and my having to lay flat for 3 months as part of the healing recovery. So many times my children stayed at her home and were just smothered in love and practical support as though they were her own children. Living 230 miles away from my natural family did not often lend itself to practical family support in any situation, but Esther, her husband John, and their children became our family in so many ways.

Now, as Esther visited, I would share the messages I had been listening to and we would have great debates as God sealed deeper understanding into both of us, taking us to a whole new level and bonding into a God-given friendship that would ultimately lead us to stand united together to serve.

However, rejection is painful, no matter how it comes about.

The isolation from friends I knew and loved, together with the attitude of my work management, which clearly affected my work colleagues in whatever was being shared at the office because no one made direct contact with me, left me cut off from people, and for a while I lived in a sense of abandonment from the masses.

Yet, even from a distance people can still have their impact on your life. Although they didn't contact me directly to maintain a relationship, people would see Esther out and about and ask how I was. It is amazing how many were shocked that I would still get into a car that Esther was driving, as though she had been responsible for the accident and how I was affected now! This made Esther feel guilty even though she wasn't, and I had to give every reassurance that I did not blame her for anything and help her to forgive herself for taking on board false guilt! People are people, and they seem to explain things by apportioning judgement and blame. Thankfully, we learned to live above it!

But, in the first instance, I didn't understand. Rejection hurts, and again, I was faced with a choice. How would I allow this to affect me? In some ways, I felt incredibly lost and alone, but as my emotions were filtered through understanding in my faith, I had to accept that everyone has a free will choice and people do not always value themselves in a relationship. What I mean is, people, do not always recognise what they bring into someone else's life. So when they withdraw, for whatever reason, they do not understand what they are doing to the other person, what they are letting go of, what they rob themselves and the other person of.

But I also began to realise that on our journey of life some people have a momentary impact, others are for a season, some become acquaintances that you connect with occasionally and you are able to pick up a thread that runs between you from wherever you last saw each other. Others are friendships of regular connection and crossover of life that allow the barriers to come down, and there is openness and honesty and value expressed in many dimensions of growth together. Some are family relationships, others are work acquaintances.

And then there are the unique, intimate, inner circle connected relationships that grow together, thrive together, encourage together, laugh together, cry together, share together, support together, journey through all the ups and downs together, disagree but reconcile together, take responsibility together, challenge together, forgive together, celebrate in success together, mourn in loss together and seek, worship and praise God together.

It took a long time on this part of my journey to understand that God was ordering my steps in relationships. I was stripped of so much in the loss of so many friendships and yet, I was given riches beyond compare with others, especially with Esther. One of the messages I watched on God TV at that time was by T.D. Jakes who said:-

"When you are going through the fire and the mess of difficult times, there are many who will fall away and drop out of your life. But when you come out of the fire into your victory, those same people will suddenly want to know you again. There are few people who will want to journey the full course through the distress, brokenness, and difficulties with you, but those who do, will stay by your side, and be raised up with you. They are God purposed and God given!"

I knew I had to let go and let God order my steps. As I leaned closer into Him the heartache of loss was eased as I learned to trust Him in all things. My tears were turned to thankfulness for the blessing of those who stayed, although, as I was later to find out, they too would change along the way.

> # REJECTION IS NOT SOMEONE WANTING YOU OUT OF THEIR LIFE. REJECTION IS SOMEONE THAT GOD WANTED OUT OF YOUR FUTURE.
>
> soshequoted | tumblr

Trust in the Lord with all your heart and lean not on your own understanding; ⁶ in all your ways acknowledge him, and he will make your paths straight.

Proverbs 3:5-6

We do not always understand God's ways. Sometimes the relationship issues that we go through seem so unfair and we are prone to ask "Why is this happening to me?" We want to be loved, we want to be friends, we do not want to be alone. But not all relationships are good for us. Some people bring some very negative impact on our lives, yet we tolerate what they do to us for fear of being alone. However, what we tolerate, dominates. Many lives are destroyed because we refuse to let go of toxic relationships and believe for something better. This is why trusting in God is so important. He knows who we need in our lives.

Part Two

Pain, Politics
and Power

4

Nothing to Defend

Over the years I would undergo numerous medical tests to try to determine what was wrong with my body. Why was I deteriorating instead of getting better? But I also had medicals for insurance purposes as Esther's car insurance company attempted to make a claim against the other driver for damages to her car and compensation for my injuries. I found all this very distressing as I was constantly evaluated and made to prove time and time again the physical pain and frailty that I was in, and that I could not move my neck in certain ways. The constant questions, the form filling, letters, telephone calls and other correspondence that was demanded of me pulled me down emotionally as I had to constantly defend my corner.

What they didn't advise was just how 'dirty' the other side would play to avoid payment, so it was a shock when I received a DVD showing they had followed me nearly every time I had left the house to go to a hospital or doctor's appointment and filmed my every movement to try to discount my claim to suffering. I was filmed by somebody standing directly in front of me, close up, someone obviously wearing a head or body camera! My family visited from overseas and were filmed entering and leaving my house and we had no idea. I had done nothing wrong, and a film cannot show what was going on in my body and the pain that I suffered in every movement.

The invasion of my privacy shattered my confidence!

I trusted no one and I didn't have the energy or the inclination to fight as I was just so ill. The claim was eventually settled for a basic whiplash injury without consideration for what it had triggered into my body that would affect me for many years to come.

Yet again I had to choose to forgive, but I also realised I was being shown something very specific about other people's reactions to my situation. I couldn't expect them to understand or to see it from my perspective; they were not the one going through it. But the negative suspicion, false accusation, and inability to make allowances for what was really happening caused a lot of emotional turmoil.

I am so thankful for the welfare benefits system that I had access to in order to help support me through the difficulties. But again, as time went on, I was constantly filling out paperwork and answering questions, having to prove my situation over and over again. The process is impersonal, character and circumstances are not addressed in their individuality. I became a number in a system having to prove that I 'ticked' the right boxes to constantly prove my entitlement. As I deteriorated over time there was little compassion, just suspicion as to whether I was telling the truth. It was difficult and demeaning, but it had to be done. Thankfully, a lady well versed in these procedures, Annie, came into my life at just the right time, to help me complete such paperwork and stand with me when refusal came, as it sometimes did, and I had to go to appeal.

I know there are those who 'play the system' but the majority of us are sincere, honest, hard-working people who have fallen on hard times, but we believe for things to get better. The few who abuse the system spoil it for everyone else who are willing to help themselves wherever they can, but in that moment, just need a little help along the way.

As I stood in faith, I was being prepared for the difficult journey ahead.

I was initially off work for seven months. Medications were changed or increased to try to control the pain and there came a point when the Occupational Health Department became involved as they constantly assessed my ability to return to work, which I was eager to do. My managers were directed to re-organise my workstation in the office to accommodate my restricted physical movement and I was advised to wear a collar support to avoid causing distress in certain neck movements that caused me so much pain.

On their advice, Esther took me to a local shop that sold 'disability aid' equipment so that I could buy a support collar for my neck. As in all things, until you need something like that, you do not appreciate or understand the help that is available. As we entered the shop we were approached by a kind, very serious, softly spoken lady in her fifties. She was very gentle and sympathetic in her approach to my needs and was very wise in her advice of what she believed would be most suitable for me to use. I didn't know there was so much choice! Having identified the right sort for me, I was measured and duly fitted with a collar that helped hold my neck in a comfortable position, and it immediately brought relief as it prevented me from moving in ways that caused such searing pain down my back and up my neck. But it was also embarrassing and made me feel very self-conscious. I hated standing out in a crowd and this would definitely attract unnecessary attention!

As a good friend who knew me so well and could sense how I was feeling, Esther decided to lighten the moment with a bit of humour by suddenly asking, "Do you provide a lead to go with the collar?" I laughed as I understood the intimation of Esther taking me for a walk like a dog, but the sales lady was absolutely mortified and shot Esther a look of disgust as if to say, How dare you say such a horrible thing?? How insensitive can you be??

As I tried to stifle my giggles, Esther then proceeded to ask, "What sort of preacher do you think you are called to be? That collar is a little big to blend in easily as a Church of England vicar!" As we both collapsed in hysterical laughter the lady looked from one to the other not knowing how to react. Her protocols of sensitivity to the less able had been shattered, and though I gave every reassurance that I could see the funny side of the situation, as we left the shop, it was very evident that she did not! We have laughed together many times since at the memory of that moment!

A date was eventually set for my return to work in November 2004, but three weeks beforehand God clearly showed me:

"Do not defend yourself!."

I could not understand why I would even have to? I had been injured in a road accident that was not my fault, my body was suffering in ways that I had no control over, I had always been under medical supervision and advice in respect of my time off work and I was desperate to get back to normal and get on with my life, especially returning to my job!

But initially, I was still frail and I would need support to slowly build up towards taking full responsibility and duties again. Occupational Health mapped out a written programme of return to work on a slow, phased return basis, doing staggered minimal hours and restricted duties. I could not drive at this point so I would be on office bound desk duties until further notice.

So, on Monday 15th November 2004, seven months after the accident, I officially returned to work. I was only rostered to do two hours, but I was excited and ready to go to the next level of recovery. I had missed seeing and relating with my work colleagues and I couldn't wait to catch up with them again. I was looking forward to doing something useful again! I appreciated that I could only do this with their extra consideration and support until I became stronger, and I really valued what they had agreed to alter around on my behalf and to give me the opportunity to do this.

But, as I walked into the office at 9 a.m. you could have cut the atmosphere with a knife!

I was greeted by the department manager, Louise, who I had previously always had a good rapport with. She was a Christian, known for her Church activities and stand for her faith and we had conversed at many levels of our faith journey together. But she also had a reputation for high professional standards and a pride in her department to stand out under her leadership, that she was aiming high to raise the profile and reputation of everything that we did to a futuristic level in communications and service standards to the public. And in this, we were not allowed to take our responsibilities lightly.

As I entered the room she was waiting by my desk. After a curt 'good morning' she began to point out what had been changed at my work station to accommodate my physical needs, and then immediately delegated paperwork that I had to process from a pile that was stored on my desk. After completing her instructions she then walked away to her office, approximately 5 metres away from my desk, and leaving her door open so she could hear and observe whatever else happened, she then left me to get on and do my work.

The office was awkwardly silent. The two clerical assistants, Jacky and Ann, with whom I had worked for many years were working with their heads down, almost afraid to look at me, and they were definitely afraid to speak to me. So if I had expected a 'Welcome back', 'We have missed you so much', 'It is so good to see you', 'How are you feeling?' or any other term of friendly welcome or heart of compassion over what I had been going through to ease me back into my work environment, I was to be sadly disappointed.

I sat down at my desk feeling awkward, embarrassed and fighting tears. And then I remembered God's words, "Do not defend yourself!" I set to work and quietly completed my tasks and silently thanked God that I was in His hands. About 10 minutes before my time was up, our manager Louise left the office to go to a meeting. As soon as the office door closed, the two clerical assistants shot up from their desks and ran over to me in tears of apology, to give me a hug, to say they had missed me, to welcome me back and find out what had been happening to me. They had been instructed before my arrival that morning to "not make a fuss!"

He was oppressed and afflicted, yet he did not open his mouth; he was led like a lamb to the slaughter, and as a sheep before its shearers is silent, so he did not open his mouth.

Isaiah 53:7

Prior to Jesus being crucified on the Cross, He endured all manner of abuse from His accusers. He was accused of lying, He was spat on, stripped naked, had a crown of thorns pressed onto his head, he was beaten, whipped mercilessly, and though his body was ripped to pieces, he was then made to carry his own heavy wooden cross on which he was to be crucified. Yet, he remained silent. He didn't complain. He didn't defend himself. He stayed focused on God's plan, for the victory beyond the Cross!

Jesus experienced and suffered through every pain and emotion that we can ever endure today. He empathises with us in our circumstances and our need. He understood what I was about to go through in the difficulties ahead, and as I was obedient to follow His example, my victory would come.

5

Stand Up

Over the next few weeks, I followed the timetable for working reduced hours, building up my physical strength and trying to comply with the directive from Occupational Health on what I could do. I was expected to advise the management at all times when I could not cope. I had to pace myself by taking breaks on a regular basis away from the task that I was given to do, so that I did not aggravate the injury in my body and cause a relapse in any way.

That was all fine in principal!

But it would only work if you are supported by someone with a heart to encourage, and a conscience to support and follow the directive with you. Sadly, that was not the case. I worked hard to complete all tasks given in the allocated time, but, I was constantly reprimanded for not meeting expectations, even when I had obviously done so. On many occasions, I was confronted in the middle of the office at separate times by both my line manager Barbara, and my department manager Louise, in loud aggressive tones, and I was accused of doing things that I had obviously not done as they were not my responsibility to do at that time. Or, I was told off for not doing things that they thought I should have done. I couldn't win either way.

Other people observed what was happening and on many occasions, they would approach me afterward, often in tears as they had such compassion for me, and they would confirm that they knew that I had not done what I was accused of. But in the middle of these difficult altercations, I did not retaliate or defend myself. Although the provocation was painful, as I remained quiet, their demeanour would become louder and more agitated and I knew they were frustrated because they could not get me to react. They would inevitably walk away in agitation and walk out of the office to calm down.

On one occasion both clerical assistants came to me in tears after one such management outburst and Jacky said, "What they are doing to you is all wrong. It is abuse. Why don't you just hit her??"

As I am six feet tall (1.83 metres) and my managers were around 5 feet 2 inches (1.57 metres) the picture conjured up in my head as I visualised that scenario made me crack up laughing. It broke the tension and I was able to explain why I could not retaliate.

Firstly, God had shown me that I should not defend myself and it was so important to me that I am obedient to what He was asking. I couldn't understand it, and I didn't like it, but I had to silently trust and know that I was in His hands.

Secondly, if I retaliated, I knew it would be used against me. I would be accused of countermanding instructions given by the authority over me. To do so would show disrespect and I would fall into their plan to accuse me of being argumentative and insubordinate. I had to show honour and respect to their authority, even if they were wrong in how they treated me.

Thirdly, if I hit them, I would be in the wrong and immediately set myself up for instant dismissal! Then they would achieve what I believed they were aiming for; to either get me to resign or to be removed from my post.

Yet, I didn't understand what I had done so wrong to be treated in this way?

The interesting thing was that Marjorie, the manager to the clerical staff, was also prone to confront in anger whenever something did not meet her expectations. Many a meeting took place in the filing cabinet area, where the clerical assistant would retaliate against Marjorie's wrong accusations, and raised voices could be heard around the office as she would defend herself.

Then, one day, as Marjorie approached her in the usual way and was looking to confront and argue with her, Jacky listened quietly at what she had to say but did not respond. Marjorie could be heard raising her voice, getting more and more agitated and louder and louder, but when Jacky gave no response, she stormed off in temper slamming the office door behind her.

As Jacky returned to her desk, she sat down with a satisfied smile on her face, looked at me and said, "I have watched you stand in such grace over these last few weeks in all wrong accusation and anger shown to you, but you never retaliated. You never lowered yourself to their standards. I realised that what I did in arguing with my manager was wrong, and it fuelled discontent between us. So, today, I thought I would do it your way. And wow, I feel so much better about what just happened. I don't care what I was just wrongly accused of, I know the truth and I am at peace!"

And in that moment I was suddenly aware that there was a bigger picture going on over my life and it would impact many other people's lives around me as they observed my journey, and they would be changed too.

As the weeks progressed the tasks allocated became more and more demanding and they highlighted the physical frailty in my neck and back. I was always honest with the managers if I had difficulty coping but I was ignored and their demands continued. As I was pushed to the limit emotionally and physically I chose to obey God and not defend myself, but always to show honour and respect no matter how wrongly I was treated. I learned to stand in grace.

Now don't get me wrong, I am no angel.

I could do the right thing in the office, but I was hurting emotionally and physically. I would go home at the end of my duties and just cry, talk it out with Esther which allowed me to be honest with myself, and to understand how I was really feeling about everything, and then I was able to give my day to God in prayer. I didn't understand what was happening, but He did! As I let go of my heartache and the injustice, choosing to forgive people for abusing me and being thankful for the support I had from my other colleagues, and Esther, the honesty I vented out loud in prayer released me to face the truth of how I felt in everything, and it set me free to be me, and as I listened to God through reading my Bible and more teaching messages, He would direct my heart for Him.

If I had bottled it all up, the emotional pain would have been buried deep inside my heart and that would have turned to bitterness, anger, and unforgiveness. The only person who would have suffered even more in all of that was me, because everyone else would have still carried on being free to be who they are, and doing what they do, but I would have been a prisoner of their behaviour, a volcano of emotions waiting to erupt sometime in the future when I least expected it.

He's closer than
you think
just a conversation
away
if only you could find
the time
to bow your head
and pray

© SOSHEQUOTED | TUMBLR

If you are feeling lost and lonely, I encourage you to talk to God. He is always listening for our heart to speak to Him so that He can show us a way forward in all things.

Unforgiveness is like drinking poison yourself and waiting for the other person to die.

Marianne Williamson

Unforgiveness always hurts us. The other person will walk away and freely get on with their lives, regardless of what they have done to us. We hold ourselves in a prison of pain and regret about many things if we are unable to forgive.

Three times I pleaded with the Lord to take it away from me. ⁹But he said to me, "My grace is sufficient for you, for my power is made perfect in weakness."

2 Corinthians 12:8-9

As we all do when going through hard times, I pleaded with God to take the difficulties away from me, to change things for the better because it was so painful and I didn't understand. But He always knew best and He gave me the grace to cope. He was my strength when I was so weak.

6

Pharaoh Incarnate

As time progressed my hours were increased until I could cope with working a full eight hour day. The tasks given became more demanding as I was taken away from just doing desk orientated paperwork and telephone duties, and was instead told to assist in a stock check and reorganisation of storage for the heavy and cumbersome communication equipment that we provided for clients.

Unfortunately, from their point of view, I could not do this task on my own. I could not climb a ladder, reach above my head, or lift/carry any more than one box of equipment at a time. When physically well, I had been able to carry three boxes at once so the task would have been so much quicker. You can therefore imagine how impatient and disgruntled my line manager Barbara became at having to first of all help me, and then work within my limitations by having to do many aspects of the job herself. It was a very tense time and her attitude constantly flared in complaint and frustration.

Again, no matter what I did I was always in the wrong, and the boundaries were crossed many times on what I should have been expected to do. I would report my concerns on many occasions, but I was always asked to carry on with the task. At one point I was suddenly asked to meet with both managers together, and I was challenged in no uncertain terms about my suitability to carry on with the job. I was slowly improving, but not quickly enough for their liking. The meeting was tense, abusive, awkward and embarrassing in many ways.

So many times I held it together at work, but I would go home in tears. I would pray and ask God for help to overcome the difficulties, for a softening of their hearts so that we could work together for the same aim: my complete recovery and restoration to continue being able to do my job.

But it seemed every time I sought that sort of resolution and asked the management for support to achieve it, they would harden their hearts even more against me. Then God showed me the parallel to Moses and his ten requests to Pharaoh, asking him to set God's people free. On each occasion that Moses asked for their release, Pharaoh hardened his heart and refused. But eventually, they got the victory!

Every time I asked for help at work, it was refused.

As we entered the fourth month after my return to work I still had to use the neck collar to avoid straining my back, and I was still being asked to do things beyond my physical capacity to cope. February was the annual billing time for my clients. This was one time of the year when the three managers, two clerical assistants and I would normally set aside everyday duties, except for anything that was urgent to be attended to, and focus together on filling approximately 3500 envelopes with invoices, record amendment sheets and any other paperwork that was intended for distribution at that time. It was a soul destroying task but by 'working together as a team' it could be done quickly and in a matter of days.

However, this year, the task was allocated for me to do it all on my own!!

I was assured that I could do it at my own pace, I could take as many breaks away from the task as I needed to if I became physically uncomfortable, and they would extend the deadline for completion to give me three weeks to complete it. There were five items of paperwork to be folded into each envelope. That equated to 17,500 pieces of paper to be handled!

It was an arduous task and they wouldn't take no for an answer!

As you can imagine, to sit at a desk folding papers into envelopes all day is a challenging task for anyone, but doing it as part of a team carries you through. To do it on my own when wearing a neck collar and suffering pain in the upper back was never going to bode well, but they wouldn't listen, and I didn't understand why. I commenced the task in hand and plodded my way through each day. As the days went on, and the repetitive strain kicked in, the discomfort built up. I was taking more breaks away from the task than I actually spent time doing it, but they didn't seem to care. All requests for help fell on deaf ears. I was desperate to keep my job so I continued to push through.

As the three-week deadline approached, I was nowhere near completing the task.

I had gone to bed night after night crying out to God for His help and direction. Then one morning I woke up early with an overwhelming urge that I had to write an email to my manager Louise. I wrote it out on my home computer and emailed it to my work email account. I simply explained that I was struggling to cope, advised her that I could not complete the task by the deadline given, and I asked if I could be released from the task or be given help to complete it.

On arrival at work I copied it into an email to Louise, but just as I was about to press the 'send' button I was prompted in my spirit to do a 'Read Report'! I had never heard of such a thing. Information Technology is not one of my strong points! But as I focused on the screen I was able to work out how to do it, and with a sense of satisfaction in that achievement, the email was duly sent.

I received a 'Read Report' email just over three hours later.

I had anticipated that Louise may telephone me immediately to advise what, if anything, she was willing to do to help, but I heard nothing from her all day. So, I carried on with the task, be it at a very slow pace! It was 24 hours later that I received an emailed reply from Louise indicating:-

I should carry on with the task.

There was no help available.

The deadline for completion would be extended.

Little did I know at that moment in time just how important, precious and life changing these three emails would become!

The task was completed three weeks later and it was a tremendous relief for me physically and emotionally. I felt very weak in all that my body had been subjected to, but I managed to hold it together. Then, as part of my continued progress, I was encouraged to consider attempting to drive again.

The journey to work was only ten minutes by car, so after a few short practice sessions over the weekend, I drove to work for the first time in eleven months on a Monday morning. I removed the collar for driving but I used it when necessary while working at my desk. I hated wearing it, and I had not wanted to become dependent on it, but it became an essential part of learning to cope.

Louise's next project was to get me out of the office doing my full-time regular duties. As she knew I had driven my car she saw no excuse for me not to go to the next level. But it was an arduous task. The bag that I had to carry was the size of an average suitcase and contained a selection of equipment to choose from according to the practicality of the client's home set up, that I could not pre-empt before visiting. Parking was not always convenient to the location I needed to be at, and the environment I had to work in for completing paperwork was an unknown quantity until I was inside their home.

However, whatever it was going to cost me to do so, I stepped back into the job that I loved! The service we provided was unique and I loved to encourage people to receive the help that was available to them, to leave them supported and knowing that somebody cared about who they were, to offer them a safety net in times of unpredictable causes for concern. Our conversations went beyond just the need for our professional services, as people felt comfortable to share their innermost hurts with me. I made time to listen to them and then encouraged them in whatever way I could so that they would know their worth beyond their circumstances.

And God was always faithful. No matter how much time I gave to the clients in their need of the moment, I always managed to do my job professionally, efficiently and successfully. I also completed everything in the time slot allocated for each person, thereby avoiding questions and negative comments that would have ensued from my managers if I had run over my time.

I loved being back in my qualified role, but the physical toll took a hold on my body very quickly.

Moving my head left to right for observation when driving was painful. Without a collar, I had no restriction to keep me within safe boundaries and not aggravate the injury. The equipment bag was so heavy to carry, and multiple forms had to be completed using a clipboard on my knee, as usually there would not be a flat surface to work on in the client's home. This meant moving my head up and down, looking at the client as I asked them questions, and then looking down to write their answer.

Inevitably this inflamed my back injury and I was very quickly brought to my knees!

On the afternoon of April 11th, 2005 I was doing my second appointment of the day, completing paperwork after the successful installation of the equipment, when I began to feel dizzy and I had difficulty focusing. I struggled through to completion, maintaining a professional presentation so that I didn't upset the elderly client. As I stood up to leave, I thought I was going to pass out, but after steadying myself, I managed to get myself back to my car.

I stood at the side of the car feeling nauseated, disorientated and unable to physically move to get into the car. I knew I would be unable to drive.

I used my mobile phone to call the office to ask for help, which was answered by Barbara in the same attitude that I had encountered when reporting sick during the seven months off work. There was no compassion, just question after question and a reluctance to help. It took some persuasion to convince her that I was not fit to drive and eventually I just hung up on the call in tears. It was 25 minutes later that a work colleague arrived to help me, although the office was only 10 minutes down the road.

Her instructions had been to pick me up and take me back to the office. I had worked with this lady for many years, and she knew my strong resolve, so one look at my grey pallor and physical distress was enough for her to know that something was radically wrong, and she made the instant decision to take me straight home. She called the office to communicate what she was going to do and Barbara was angry in her protest, "If she was that ill she should call an ambulance and go to the hospital."

All I needed to do, was to get home and lay down to relieve the stress in my body. I was assisted into my colleague's car and taken straight home, regardless of the consequences with management. That colleague was my life saver, and I will be ever grateful for her compassionate support and courage to stand up on my behalf.

After only five months since the return to my job, that day was the last time I would work for a very long time.

I was about to enter into a new phase of the journey that would be part of changing my life forever!

> ²⁶"So do not be afraid of them, for there is nothing concealed that will not be disclosed, or hidden that will not be made known. ²⁷What I tell you in the dark, speak in the daylight; what is whispered in your ear, proclaim from the roofs. ²⁸Do not be afraid of those who kill the body but cannot kill the soul. Rather, be afraid of the One who can destroy both soul and body in hell.
>
> Matthew 10:26-28

I was reassured through these verses that I had nothing to fear, and though it seemed that what had been happening would go unnoticed, there would be a point sometime in the future when the truth would be revealed. All I was being asked to do was to speak up, tell the truth at all times, stand firm in how God was directing my journey and though my body was suffering, I knew I would not be destroyed as a person. But only God could show me how, and by faith, I had to stay so close to Him.

7

Angels – Human

After a long night of painkillers and broken sleep, feeling crushed in spirit and struggling physically, I contacted the Occupational Health Department to advise what had happened the day before. I was given an appointment for the following day to see them urgently, but I was asked to email a report of the incident to them as soon as possible. I had been monitored month by month during my return to work, and they had repeatedly cautioned my management that they were deviating from the Occupational Health instructions that had been given to protect me.

I had never met Dr. Hayes before, but as he considered my file, carried out a physical assessment and then completed his report, he had no hesitation in stating to my employer that they, and my departmental manager Louise, were responsible for my collapse. They had not adhered to or upheld the guidelines given in order to support me in my safe return to work. As a direct consequence of allocating tasks for me to complete that were far beyond the accepted boundaries for my continued recovery, they had compounded my physical frailty and incapacitation.

I received the report in the post and, as I read it, I just crumbled emotionally.

I was thankful for the truth exposed, but I so loved my job, and I knew there was no way back into it from this point on. I was absolutely devastated as that truth sank in. What was I going to do? I needed to work; I had a mortgage to pay! A battle was about to commence that I didn't want to be part of. I didn't like politics, I hated being singled out, I disliked being the centre of attention, especially as I knew I would be wrongly accused on a bigger public platform. I feared what my employers would do. I didn't know what would happen; I didn't know where to turn! Except to stand on my faith and go to God in prayer!

I knew I could not do this alone. I needed someone who knew employment law and would stand up for my rights. I had never considered joining a union and didn't even know if they could do anything to help, but I was led to contact one now. The door immediately opened and I was put into contact with Carol, a larger than life lady who was confident in who she was (unlike me), who did not mince her words (tact and diplomacy were not always her strong point) and had a driving force like a battle tank going through a minefield, exploding and exposing everything that got in her path!

We couldn't have been more different in character (I was quiet, unassuming and considerate to others before my own need; she was loud, demanding and forthright) in temperament (I was usually calm and would respond after due consideration of things; she was reactive in a moment), and in demeanour (I was submissive and didn't like to rock the boat; she was loud and confrontational).

But, she was my angel sent from Heaven, and I knew I had been given the best! The first of a few meetings with my employer, team management, and Human Resources took place and Carol had no doubt about what she was going to do and say. I was more tentative and wanted to listen to what they had to say. The physical frailty and limitations were obvious to those who chose to see, but I was asked to spell it all out and explain my side of events since returning to work.

I wasn't surprised to find out that the report from Dr. Hayes at Occupational Health was being denied, but I was shocked to find that they had sacked him from carrying out any more medicals on their behalf! As management colluded together behind the lies of my manager, who was insistent that I would not accept the help that she had offered, that I would not listen to instruction and I had repeatedly caused tension and upset in the office, things became quite heated between them and Carol. I sat quietly in a state of shock and resisted the urge to break down in tears at the injustice.

Carol was livid with the outcome and was gearing herself up for battle. Over the next few months I was on pain relief medication, would have further medical investigations to determine why my body was becoming so frail, and constant assessment by Occupational Health to monitor whether I was fit for work, not just for my original job role, but for any other position that might be available.

As we approached each meeting with my employer Carol was in fighting mode, but before each one, I knew as I sought God that I was being directed in the way that I should go. I knew that God was closing the door on my job. He was pulling me out of full-time employment for a reason. At that time I did not understand the whys and wherefores of it all, but I had an inner peace over that possibility, despite the turmoil at the injustice I encountered.

In our conversations together before we entered the room, I would caution Carol in her anger, and as they continued to stand on the lies promoted by my manager, Carol wanted to insist that I be transferred to another position in another department. But I knew before their constant refusal of that request that the door was closed, and I was at peace about it.

I was also advised that I had many grounds on which to sue my employer for the abuse I had suffered, but God said 'No'. Carol didn't understand why I was so adamant not to do so. She didn't have any faith considerations so it was difficult for her to understand how I knew what God was showing me, but she honoured how I stood so firmly in the truth that I knew, and she eventually, reluctantly, let the idea go.

It would have been very easy to go down that road as I had been so mistreated. But every day of continuing in that battle meant re-living it over and over again. It would have taken over my life in the preparation for court proceedings and left me forever having to defend and prove myself, keeping me so focused in the past that I would not be able to live in freedom in the present. For many years as it was being pursued, I would have been trapped in a prison in my emotions, encountered further abuse, and risked losing all sense of my identity by becoming the victim of something so poisonous, vindictive and destructive, that I didn't want any part of it. And in the end, no matter what the financial settlement might have been, it would not have brought any joy, sense of achievement or fulfilment to my life, but may well have left me with a bitter spirit in rejection and heartache that would poison my life forever. There was a battle going on, but the battle belonged to God and I knew that one day vindication would come through His hands, His way, in-keeping with His plans for my life!

We eventually came to a stand-off point. Occupational Health would not clear me as fit to return to my original job role, but they felt that perhaps there was something else I could do, as they knew there were other vacancies I could perhaps be transferred to. My employer wouldn't consider a change of job role. In their eyes, I was either fit to work at my employed position, or I was not. If I was not fit to work, it was unfortunate, but I should perhaps resign.

Up until now, Occupational Health had not seen my employer and management team face to face, so in March 2006, eleven months after I had collapsed at work, they called us all together with Carol, my Union Representative, to attend a meeting at their offices.

As I prayed the night before the meeting, I was suddenly reminded of something that God had shown me to do many months before.

When we all arrived and took our seats in the room provided, I was instructed by Pam, the lady officiating the meeting on behalf of Occupational Health, that, as I was in so much pain, if I felt uncomfortable I had her permission to stand up and freely move around at any point in the meeting without feeling embarrassed to do so. I thanked her, took my seat and the meeting began.

As questions were asked of Louise my manager, to explain her actions towards my situation, she spoke very eloquently with a sure attitude that she would not be defied or defeated. While being taken step by step through the report I had submitted immediately after my collapse, she confidently defended her position turning everything against me, clearly stating that I was uncooperative and disruptive.

I could see Carol was beginning to quietly seethe but she didn't say a word. I stood up to stretch out and relieve the pain building up in my body and I turned my back on everyone to do so, as my emotions were about to get the better of me. But, then I heard the question asked, "When Grace had repeatedly asked you for help when she had difficulty carrying out the tasks that you gave her, why did you refuse?"

Louise confidently replied, "At no time did she ever ask me for help."

At that point, I turned to face them all again and I quietly asked if I could say something. Before speaking, I opened up an envelope that I had brought with me to the meeting through God's prompting the night before. I was then able to produce the three emails that I had printed off when I had asked for help to complete the annual billing. I read my email aloud, clearly stating the time and date it was sent. I then read the time and date of the 'read report' email. Then I read the reply that I had received 24 hours later, where help was refused, I had been instructed to carry on with the task on my own, and the completion deadline was to be extended to enable me to do so.

Louise became very agitated, sat forward on the edge of her seat and began to aggressively raise her voice against me in her defence. Her manager, Mr. Davidson, sat back in his chair, rolled his eyes to the ceiling in dismay, and conceded defeat as her lies were exposed. Pam from Occupational Health tried to calm things down, but when unable to do so, she stood up, asked me to take a seat with Carol, then she took Louise by the arm, and as she continued in full angry verbal rant, she physically escorted her and Mr. Davidson not only out of the room, but also out of the building!!

In that one moment, by the grace of God, I was fully vindicated from all wrong accusation!

Pam came back into the room, appalled at what had just been witnessed, but with a spring in her step at the victory just won. Checking that I was alright, she reassured me that everything would be okay. Her report would be submitted immediately and Human Resources would be in touch as soon as possible. Carol was elated and almost danced her way out of the office. I was shaken at the verbal outburst from someone who I had admired and looked up to for so many years, someone who was always so upright and pro-fessional, but who, today, had shown her true colours and fallen from grace.

I also sensed that the battle was far from over!

And I was right. Their immediate response after that meeting was for them to contact Carol, and through her, offer me a job in another department on a lower pay scale.

Carol believed this was a good thing as at least I would be still employed. Also, if I refused to take it, I would end up with nothing, because now that they had made an offer to me, I was put in the position of either accepting it or having to resign. It was Friday afternoon; I was told I had until Monday to respond with a decision.

I knew that there was absolutely no way that I could take that job offer. I was aware that not to do so would leave me unemployed, but God would not give me any peace towards it. I had no idea what the future held, I just knew, that I knew, that I knew, that it was so wrong and I could not accept it. But how was I to convince Carol, who had worked so hard on my behalf, that now, in what seemed like a victory outcome for her to secure something of a job position for me, I would have to turn it down?

I prayed hard all weekend, fearing her response to my decision and pleading with God to help me to stand my ground with her one more time. I knew she would be upset, disappointed and frustrated with my stand, particularly as I was again led by God, and as an unbeliever, Carol would not comprehend how or why. I asked God to prepare her heart to receive what I had to say.

Carol contacted me first thing Monday morning to ask if she could come to visit me at home. This was unusual as every other meeting, no matter how frail I had been, had always meant my having to go to her office. I had been told that home visits were not allowed. I was surprised, but I agreed she could come over. And I prayed desperately for the right words to convey what I knew. As I answered the door she breezed in past me as though she owned the place, choosing to sit at the dining table and not on the couch.

I joined her and she immediately declared, "You cannot take that job!"

I was shocked, stunned and elated that she was in agreement with what I knew to be true without me having to say a word, but I was overwhelmed at God answering my prayers in such a profound way, and I was momentarily speechless. She continued to explain her stance, that I was being subjected to continued manipulation, control and abuse by my managers, and if I was to continue working, she believed that I should be deployed in another department on a job scale at least equivalent to what I was now earning, or, because of the abuse I had been subjected to, I should be promoted in some way to a higher position.

As I pulled myself together, I confirmed my agreement that I could not accept their job offer, as God had already shown me that I could not do so. Carol sat forward on her chair, slammed the palm of her hand down with such force on the table top that it shook violently, and I nearly jumped out of my skin with shock. Then she yelled at me, "How do you know what God is saying to you? In every meeting in recent months, you have restrained my approach because of what you say 'God has shown you'. I just do not understand how you can know what God is saying."

As I re-composed myself, I picked up my Bible that was already on the table, and with God's leading and grace I was able to show her different scriptures that had guided me at different points of the journey and piece together the puzzle in her understanding. She listened attentively and was absolutely mesmerised at the intimacy of God and was so touched that tears welled up in the awe of it all. This beautiful lady who is normally so bolshy and brash was touched in the love of God and didn't know what to do.

God had caused our paths to cross for such a time as this. Carol brought something very powerful and special into my life as she had stood in my defence. In this moment, she encountered the powerful intimacy of God and would be changed forever. We came to an agreement on the way forward regarding my job, trusting God together for the outcome once I had refused their offer.

As she left the house I was able to do what I had been shown by God to do a few weeks earlier. I gave her a Bible that I had bought for her as a 'thank you, for her professional support. I didn't know how I was going to give it without crossing professional standards, but God brought her into my home to bring down the dividing barrier between us, and she graciously accepted the gift explaining that she would now go to Church with her sister-in-law, who had invited her on many occasions, but she had never wanted to go, until now.

> **In your anger do not sin: Do not let the sun go down while you are still angry,**
>
> **Ephesians 4:26**

Anger doesn't solve anything. Once a voice is raised all authority is lost, the recipient cannot hear the words spoken because of the aggressive nature in which they are being delivered and it causes such provocation and distraction.

> **[1] Listen to my prayer, O God,**
> **do not ignore my plea;**
> **[2] hear me and answer me.**
> **My thoughts trouble me and I am distraught**
> **[3] because of what my enemy is saying,**
> **because of the threats of the wicked;**
> **for they bring down suffering on me**
> **and assail me in their anger.**
>
> **Psalm 55:1-3**

This was my heart's cry so many times in prayer as I pleaded with God over my situation. I was troubled and distraught because of the lies told and the threats made against me in anger from the management. All I wanted was to hear God's voice and know what He wanted me to do.

I cry out to God Most High,
to God, who vindicates me
³ He sends from heaven and saves me,
rebuking those who hotly pursue me
God sends forth his love and his Faithfulness

Psalm 57:2-3

My God is faithful and loves me so much. I knew one day I would be vindicated and saved from all wrong accusation as He exposed all those who stood against me.

8

Angels – Supernatural

As Carol advised my employer that I was refusing to accept the offer of the new job position, I was initially advised to submit my resignation in writing. But later that day I received a telephone call from Wendy in Human Resources, who brought a sudden and very surprising twist to the events.

Firstly, after a brief discussion to assess my welfare, I received an unexpected 'off the record' apology for the 'disgusting way' that I had been treated over the last two years. Wendy had only just taken up her new role in Human Resources and had today been given my file. If she had been in post throughout my journey she would not have allowed me to be treated in this way. I was overwhelmed with her compassion and concern for my situation.

Secondly, Wendy was of the opinion that I was not to submit my resignation, but we should explore the possibility that I might be able to be retired on 'ill health grounds'. To do so, I had to consent to be assessed by two individual doctors, who would both have to agree that I was unfit to work. If I was prepared to go down that road, she would immediately put the wheels in motion to complete it as soon as possible. I duly consented, and within two days I received a letter advising the date of the first appointment planned in two weeks time.

God had a plan, and His timing is always perfect.

On April 12th, 2006 at 0900 hours I attended that appointment at the Occupational Health Department offices. I had been there on many previous occasions in the last two years, so I was very familiar with the setup and where I should go. I entered the reception area at 0850 hours but there wasn't anybody else there, not even a receptionist. I took a seat and waited patiently for someone to arrive. It was too early in the morning for my body to cope; I was in raging pain in my neck, back, arms and chest through the physical exertion to get up and be there so early.

A door opened to the room where I had always had my assessments carried out and someone stepped out and called my name saying "I think you have an appointment with me this morning." As I approached the door I came face to face with a very professional looking black gentleman who was immaculately dressed in a three-piece suit with white shirt and a tie. My first thought was to consider, why don't all doctors dress in this way? He just looked so radiant, clean, fresh and competent.

I was advised to take a seat and I could see that my file, about 7cm thick with a compilation of reports from the last two years, was unopened on the desk. The doctor apologised that due to the early appointment time he had not yet had time to read anything from my file. My heart sank as I was in so much pain, and I realised that the appointment could take a while to complete.

I then offered to give a short summary of what had been happening to bring him up to speed. He agreed, and listened carefully as I simply explained that in May 2004 I was a front seat passenger in a car that was involved in a simple rear shunt accident. I received severe whiplash, I was off work for seven months, I returned to work for five months before collapsing on 11th April 2005, and I have not been able to work since due to continued deterioration in my body.

He opened the cover of my file and studied the first page which had my name, address and job title on it. There was silence for quite a while as he contemplated the page he was looking at and my summary of events, and then without looking at me, he asked a question:

"Are you considering suing your employer?"

I was a little surprised at a doctor asking such a question, but I was hurting too much to care, so I told him, "No, I had no intention of suing my employer. Today was all about drawing a line under my past and leaving it behind me, claiming freedom to step forward into my future, whatever that might hold."

He thought for a while, and again, without looking up at me, he then asked another question:

"After the way you have been treated by your employer, which must have been very difficult and upsetting for you, do you think you need counselling?"

I was in raging pain and I wanted to get through this appointment as quickly as possible; suddenly, a boldness came over me that I didn't usually have, and I found myself saying:

"No thank you, I do not need counselling. If I can be totally honest with you, I am a Christian, a born again believer and follower of Jesus Christ. He has been my perfect counsellor throughout the whole of this journey. He has been my protector and provider and through Him, I have been brought to a place of forgiveness towards everyone, for whatever has been said or done wrong to me in the last two years. I am totally healed in my emotions, in my heart, and in my spirit. So no thank you, I do not need counselling. As I said before, today is all about drawing a line under my past and claiming freedom to step forward into my future, whatever that might hold."

At that moment he closed my file, swung round on his office chair, and for the first time since I had taken my seat, he looked me in the eye with a beaming grin and said, "Isn't our God good!"

I was stunned, but then so excited as I smiled back at him. This man knew who my Jesus is; he was a Christian too!

The next forty-five minutes have got to go on record as the most special, precious, exciting and reassuring moments of my life as we continued to converse together. As the doctor asked me questions, I was able to share many aspects of my faith journey during the last few years, not only because of the road accident, but many encounters I had enjoyed as God had ordered my steps, spoken so intimately into my life and transformed and changed me through the journey. He literally drew me into sharing my testimony with him and, as I spoke, he affirmed many things that I was saying.

As the appointment came to a close, he told me that I should write a book. I said I had just begun to do so and, as he stood up, he smiled. Looking at the name on the cover of my file, he said he would be looking out for this name on the news-stands, but then very quickly corrected himself saying, actually, that is not the name you will use to write your books. You should use your God given name, 'Grace.'

I was excited and amazed!. For weeks prior to this day, I had been challenged about my name, and was asking God to confirm if I was supposed to use my God given name 'Grace' as my author name? Now, in this moment, He had answered profoundly and I was blown away at His intimacy and confirmation, even through a doctor's appointment!

The appointment concluded with him shaking my hand, wishing me well, and stating that he would be recommending that I should be released from my employment on ill-health grounds. The receptionist still wasn't at her desk as I left the office. I was still in pain but I was elated after such a powerful appointment. Though I knew I had to see a second doctor, I was confident for the way forward.

On the way home, the friend who had offered transport to the appointment wanted to go to the local Christian book shop before dropping me home. As we pulled up outside the shop front there was a poster in the window, and as I read it, I was prompted to buy it. I went inside to purchase it, but I was told they had run out of stock. I explained that I knew I had to have it, so the lady kindly conceded and gave me the one from the window. That poster became a constant reminder in times to come that I was in God's hands, and how I might feel didn't matter.

Two weeks later I was back at the same office to see the second doctor....or so I thought!

After booking in with the receptionist, I entered the room when called, and met another doctor who clearly advised the procedure I was to go through for assessment to be retired on ill-health grounds. He stated that "Today, you are to have your first medical, and then you will be seen at a later date by someone else."

I politely pointed out that I had already seen a doctor two weeks before for my first assessment, so this was my second appointment. He checked my file and stated again, "No, this is your first medical. There is nothing on file to show you have seen anybody else."

I again reiterated that I had seen someone, in this office, just two weeks before. He again disputed my claim. As I felt so strongly about it, he went to the receptionist to check appointment records for the previous month. On his return, he advised that there was no record of my visit two weeks ago. I was dumbfounded and confused. As I submitted to the assessment with this doctor all I could think was, 'So who did I entertain for you in this office two weeks ago, God?'

As I did so, I was reminded of a verse in the Bible and I shuddered:

Do not forget to show hospitality to strangers, for by so doing, some people have shown hospitality to angels without knowing it.

Hebrews 13:2

The doctor completed his assessment and came to the conclusion that he was not happy to consent for me to be retired on ill-health grounds. Although he accepted that I was not fit to return to work immediately, he felt that given time, my body could heal and I would be able to return to work. He elected that I should be reassessed again in six months time. I left the office distraught at his decision and confused as to how this could possibly happen. I had been deteriorating and suffering in pain for two years now without improvement; what was he expecting to happen?

As I sought God in prayer, He showed me to write down everything that had happened on the previous appointment. As the Holy Spirit reminded me of the detail in the conversation I had enjoyed with the first 'doctor', I wrote down what I now understand to be a conversation with God through an Angel. A supernatural Angel!

It was a summary of my journey so far, that confirmed I was hearing God clearly and there was a call over my life as I surrendered to His will. I was overwhelmed with the intimacy of His voice and the reality check that there was so much going on in His plan for my life that I didn't yet comprehend. But I was reassured through this conversation that God was affirming and confirming my understanding of how He was leading me through all things, and as I trusted and obeyed, He would complete what He had started.

Only in reassessing the conversation did I ask questions:

- When the 'doctor' had asked if I intended to sue my employer....why would he consider that I might have grounds to do so?

- When he had asked if I needed counselling because of the way that I had been treated, which must have been very upsetting….how did he know?

In my brief summary of events at the start of the meeting I had not mentioned anything about the abuse I had encountered, and he had not read my file. But God knows EVERYTHING!

I was also remembering that he had not carried out a physical examination or made any notes when I was with him.

And where was the receptionist on that day? There was no one at the desk, (which is never usually left unattended during office hours), at the time of my arrival or departure? It was almost as though time had come to a standstill in an isolated bubble, away from the crowd.

For we are God's handiwork, created in Christ Jesus to do good works, which God prepared in advance for us to do.
Hebrews 2:10

We are all created by God and He has given us unique characters and talents that He will use to do the things that He has planned for us to do. But we have a choice whether to include Him in our lives or to live life our way. If we follow God He will show us His plan, but we always have a choice – to do it His way – or our way.

being confident of this, that he who began a good work in you will carry it on to completion until the day of Christ Jesus.
Philippians 1:6

I was confident that I was in God's hands and what He had begun in my life, He would bring to completion. But

I had to go through the journey with Him, trusting Him and being obedient to what He was asking me to do as He led me step by step. This journey will go on for the rest of my life!

It would be seven months later before I was recalled by Human Resources to be reassessed again. My physical capacity had not improved at all in that time. I was contacted on a Friday afternoon by an apologetic Wendy, who said they had overrun on the appointment plan of a six-month check-up. They had an appointment booked for Tuesday afternoon, was I able to attend? If not, we had to wait another month.

As I entered the room for the appointment on Tuesday afternoon I was pleasantly surprised to come face to face with Doctor Hayes (the doctor previously sacked for blaming my manager for my collapse). He began to explain the procedure again and said he would be doing my first assessment today. He didn't remember seeing me before. I explained when and how we had met, and reminded him that he had written a letter to my management in April 2005. He found his letter on my file, read it through and smiled. He then confirmed that he had been sacked from doing medicals for my employer as a result of this report.

So, how come he was here today? They had contacted his office urgently on Friday when they realised my appointment was overdue. He was the only one available to do an urgent appointment, so they had agreed he could do it. He then stated that in three weeks time he was moving back to his native country to work. If I had waited a month I would have missed him!

After completing a thorough examination Dr. Hayes conceded that, in his opinion, there was no other way to go, but to recommend my release from employment on ill health terms. However, because he had seen me on a previous occasion he could not be the first doctor to sign my report. He would therefore discuss my case with a colleague, and if they agreed to sign as the first consent, he would countersign the report in agreement, and I would be released without seeing another doctor.

He asked me to give him a moment to write out his report. As I was in radical discomfort he suggested I walk around the office until he had finished. As I walked around the room I saw a screen saver message on his laptop and I wanted to cry. The message was a verse from the Bible. This man was a Christian too! God had resurrected him back into place to complete what He had started through him in April 2005!

I was again overwhelmed at the miracle working ways of God.

This was the verse I saw on the screen saver:

A cheerful heart is good medicine,
but a crushed spirit dries up the bones.
Proverbs 17:22.

To live a life in joy gives us all hope, to be happy despite our circumstances is powerful, and it helps us to overcome difficulties, but if we are crushed in our spirit we lose our drive, our focus, our purpose, and this can be so damaging and it affects our choices.

For the Lord Almighty has purposed, and who can
thwart him?
His hand is stretched out, and who can turn it back?
Isaiah 14:27

God was showing me that no man would stop His plans being actioned into our lives!

It would be another five months before the formalities would be completed that allowed me to be formally released from my employment. It was a day of mixed emotions. I had worked with them for 13 years, but there was no collection, no flowers and no formal send off by my colleagues. I was just quietly dismissed as though I never existed.

As I look back now on the journey to final release, I often think 'if only I had realised that God had wanted to remove me from full-time employment, I would have willingly surrendered and let Him have His way.' But life isn't like that. I didn't understand at the time and I fought to keep it as I thought it was the only way I could survive. The journey was intense, it was painful, it was challenging. But today, I look back and realise just how much I have changed because of the experience.

How I have learned to stand up for what I believe to be right, to confront in truth, to trust God in every detail of my life, to surrender to let God have His way, to be thankful in all things despite the circumstances, to forgive quickly, and most of all, how I have learned to believe in and experience the miracle working ways of God as He does what only He can do. Nothing is impossible for Him!

I am so thankful for the angels, supernatural and human, that He brought alongside me to help in every way possible. I was never alone. He ordered my steps and brought me through to victory. The release was God's way to provide a small income for life and to set me on a road of belief for what was to happen next. The best was yet to come. But how?

If you say, "The Lord is my refuge,"
and you make the Most High your dwelling,
no harm will overtake you,
no disaster will come near your tent.
For he will command his angels concerning you
to guard you in all your ways;

Psalm 91:9-11

God is my refuge and I have chosen to live my life with Him. Whatever happens around me I will be enabled by Him to cope through all circumstances. His angels, supernatural and human, will guard me, help me, and support me in and through everything.

Jesus looked at them and said, "With man this is impossible, but with God all things are possible."
Matthew 19:26

There was nothing that I or anyone else could have done to bring about the eventual outcome of this journey. But with God, nothing is impossible! Whatever we are going through, whatever the trauma, illness, financial limitations, relationship breakdowns etc, it may seem impossible to believe for anything good to come out of the difficulties. But when we include God in the journey, when we ask Him what He thinks, He speaks to us, He leads us, He enables us, He helps us and NOTHING IS IMPOSSIBLE in his hands.

This is the poster I purchased from the Christian Book shop.

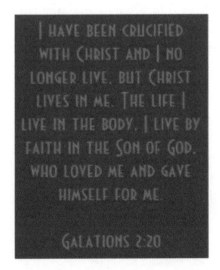

As I took these words to heart, I couldn't help but consider that I was being asked to surrender my life totally to God, letting go of everything that I might think my life was going to be, and to follow His plan into all that I was being called to be for Him.

I prayed, I surrendered. I knew that whatever was ahead, I was in His hands and God is faithful.

But it costs to serve God!

This was a life changing decision. Everything about my future was about to change because I was no longer going to make decisions based on what I wanted, or what I expected to happen. I would trust God implicitly and let Him order my life to bring me into a position to do what He was asking me to do. I wouldn't always understand His ways, but whatever I had to give up, to learn everything about who He is, and to claim what he has planned for my life, I was prepared to let Him have His way.

We cannot keep doing the same things and expect situations to change. To 'have' something different, we have to 'do' something different.

PART THREE

CONFUSION, HEALING
& DETERIORATION

9

I Believe

Now that I was no longer employed and the emotional stress of the battle with my employers was over, I became dependent on God in a whole different way. My financial situation had changed drastically, I was living in my own home with all the usual bills to pay, but my income was very low. I stayed focused on the discipline I had maintained for the last two years of listening to Christian teaching, and to read my Bible, and to seek God in everything. He never ceases to amaze me in the ways that He answers my prayers.

Suddenly, I received an offer from someone who was willing to take over the mortgage on my house, to enable me to be relieved of the responsibility, but to allow me to continue living in the home. By now, my two sons were living independently, so it was only my 17-year-old daughter and myself who lived there. A contract was duly drawn up and the house became co-owned, protecting my investment. I had a student come to live with us for a while, so with the extra income, I could afford to pay the other running costs.

Medically, my body required constant help with medication, rest, and the continued use of the neck collar when necessary for support. On one occasion a locum doctor prescribed a new tablet to ease my pain. I was aware that each tablet had side effects, and after three weeks of taking this particular tablet, I wasn't feeling good. I just felt so low, isolated and closed down, even with other people around me. I also had dark thoughts that came crashing in around me one night as I tried to sleep. This over-riding urge came over me, tempting me to take my life. I had the means to do it, the tablets were strong. I knew it was wrong, yet I couldn't shake the thoughts from my head. I couldn't do anything except cry out through my tears for help. I kept repeating in my head one name, 'JESUS, JESUS, JESUS'.

And then, at 2 a.m. my telephone rang. I picked it up, though I couldn't speak. But then, I didn't have to. The caller was my friend's son Billy, who also believed in Jesus. He was out in London for the night and had an overwhelming urge to call me, and as I listened he began to pray and speak the power of Jesus over my life. For the next two hours, he just ministered God's truths into my spirit and carried me through the dark hours of the night. The suicidal thoughts disappeared as the love of God overwhelmed me. Billy's obedience to pick up the telephone that night saved my life!

The following morning I went back to see my doctor. He was livid when he saw what I had been prescribed by the locum doctor. The tablet was a good one to have, but I had been prescribed three times the safe dose to use. One of the known side effects was depression. The overdose compounded the problem and could have cost me my life.

But God had other plans.

A few months later, on 26th January 2008, I received another telephone call from Billy. This time, he was attending a Bible college in California. He called me at 0800 hrs UK time to ask me one question: "Did I have the faith to believe that if he took me to the healing rooms at Bethel Church, linked up via Skype, and someone prayed for me, that I could be healed?"

I said "Yes," so he told me he would call me back via Skype in eight hours time.

I had a sense of excitement and bewilderment as I began my day. Then I decided, if I am going to have a 'God encounter' I want to know something has really happened, so I didn't take any painkillers. Eight hours later I was raging in pain in my neck, upper back and down my arms, when I received Billy's call on Skype. He was outside the building and wanted to know that we had a connection before he went in. As he entered I could hear the conversation between him and his friends as they asked him what he was doing there.

"I have brought my friend for healing," he said.

"Where are they?" They asked.

"She is here on my laptop," he said.

Then someone said, "Oh, we have never done this before."

A continued hub of conversation took place between them, then suddenly, two ladies appeared on my screen. They had the faith to believe that this was the right thing to do. Ann and Lynn introduced themselves to me, and as we talked they asked if I could turn on my webcam. I did so, reluctantly, because I was so camera shy. As my face came up on their screen they both gave a startled reaction and exclamations of "Oh my goodness!" Now, I know I am not photogenic, but I didn't think I looked that bad, did I? I was later to find out that as my face appeared on screen they could see a radiant white aura around my head and it had startled them.

For the next half hour, a conversation took place where these two ladies, who are total strangers to me, both began to tell me things that God had shown me during the past seven years. Billy didn't know these details, so they didn't learn them from him. This was God, through the power of the Holy Spirit, showing His presence with us. It was so exciting, but the intimacy of detail was overwhelming.

Eventually, I was asked what I needed healing for. I explained that I was suffering from whiplash as a result of a car accident, that I had pain in my back and neck. I could not put my chin down towards my chest or rotate my neck more than 5 cm to the left or right. One lady turned her back to the screen and the other one traced on her back the areas that she felt I was referring to as my problem.

I was alone in the room, sitting with my laptop at the end of my dining table. I was asked if I believed that God was with me in the UK, and also with them in California. As I agreed, I was encouraged to close my eyes and do nothing else except to believe. I wasn't to speak, pray or do anything else, except to be prepared to receive whatever God was going to do for me.

I closed my eyes and relaxed, expectant, but not knowing what would happen. Ann then simply prayed, "Lord, whatever went out of alignment in Grace's spine at the point of impact in the car accident, would you please realign it now, for your glory."

I immediately felt as though someone else came up from behind me in the room, and put both their hands firmly around my neck. As they did so, I heard an audible cracking sound, felt something move in the back of my head from up behind the lower skull, my ears popped and a warmth ran down my neck. From that moment on I was able to rotate my head fully to the left and to the right, and I could touch my chin to my chest.

As soon as the ladies saw me move my head from side to side, the Skype signal crashed, and we were unable to get re-connection. But my neck was healed! I could freely move it and I would no longer need to use the neck collar for support. I eventually gained a telephone connection with Billy and confirmed to him that my neck was healed. He was ecstatic and would convey the message to Ann and Lynn. They then explained, that as soon as they had seen the radiant white 'aura' around my head when my face first came up on the screen, they had known that God was present in the moment, and He was about to do something powerful!

There was no doubt whatsoever that my neck was healed! I had been through many medical examinations in the last four years including neck X-rays, but I had never been diagnosed as having any problems with my spine. Obviously, something had been out of alignment and had caused me to have such distress, but not anymore.

It was so obvious to everyone that something had happened as I no longer needed to wear the neck collar for support. I shared what God had done for me with so many people over the coming months. It was a real encouragement to many that through Jesus, God was still miraculously healing people today! All for the glory of His name!

And my God will meet all your needs according to the riches of his glory in Christ Jesus.
Philippians 4:19

There is no limit to what God can do for us. Whatever our need is, physically, emotionally, practically, financially or otherwise, God is bigger than the problem!

We need to tell our 'problem' how big our God is, not tell God how big our problem is!

Lord my God, I called to you for help, and you healed me.
Psalm 30:2

With the faith of two ladies 8000 miles away, we called out to God in faith, and He healed me.

10

How Can This Be Happening?

The healing of my neck was miraculous and could never be denied. But as time went on I was aware that I still had some pain in the middle of my back, and over the next few months, it began to increase and to spread all over my body.

Many people were asking how this could happen. If God is all powerful, and if He has healed my neck, why has He not healed the pain in my back? The honest answer was, 'I didn't know!' I didn't like what was happening, but I also knew that I didn't have to defend His ways. I continued to trust regardless of what the circumstances looked like.

By August 2008 my balance became so poor that I couldn't walk in a straight line. People commented that I walked like a drunk, but they knew I didn't drink! Even strangers in the supermarket commented that I should "take more water with it." My legs became weak and painful, I developed a tremor in my arms, the pain spread across my chest and into my arms, hands, and fingers. I have to admit, I didn't understand what was happening and I didn't like it. I didn't understand God's ways.

I was struggling more and more to cope on my own. I had supported and encouraged my daughter to go to university as I did not want to interfere with plans for her life. I was not her responsibility. I did not want my children or anybody else to be restricted by what was happening to me. But living alone was becoming a hazard and as Esther and her husband monitored from a distance, they were led by God to invite me to move into their home where they could keep an eye on me.

This was one of those steps that you take in blind faith, being thankful for the help being offered as it relieved so much stress. I then no longer had to struggle with domestic chores and cooking etc, but we were stepping into the unknown, the bigger picture of life that you cannot see. Only as you live day to day can you see it unfold, and you are so thankful for the blessing, but you question what it is all about.

Esther willingly helped out with attending hospital appointments as I went through numerous medical investigations to try to find out what was wrong with me. As time went on I could see that this was all part of God's continued provision for my life, but I did not want her to take on board a responsibility that was not hers to carry. I could see it was also part of God's testing, training and equipping for me, Esther and her husband John, on what was to come, as He prepared us all for a future together to serve Him.

I don't usually argue with God as He is always right! Unlike Esther, who frequently prayer walks when out with her dog and 'strops' things out with God that she doesn't like or understand, and questions what He is doing! But, I have to admit to having my own two-week strop with God in October of that year as my body deteriorated.

Every day, for many years now, I would have a prayer time on my own in the bedroom, talking to God about everything that was a cause for concern, praising Him for everything He was in my life, thankful for all that He was doing, and listening as He gave answers and direction over all that I surrendered to Him. But suddenly, for two weeks, I began to protest against Him in attitude.

I complained that I did not understand His ways. He had healed my neck miraculously 10 months earlier, and I had shared testimony, to the glory of His name, with so many people who had been encouraged to believe in Him for themselves through what He had done for me. But, I argued, with all that was going on in my body right now, especially the head to foot chronic pain that was intensifying; I wanted to know, "How did this glorify Him?"

I continued in this question for two weeks, and then, God gave me His answer one day at a church prayer meeting. I was approached by a young man called Leon who said, "Grace, God has told me to tell you that He does not need you to glorify Him!"

Ouch! I reeled at the rebuke I had just had spoken to me. My thoughts went all over the place at the power of his words. How did Leon know what I had been protesting to God about in my private prayer time? It was as though he had been a fly on the wall in my room. But I also knew I had been reprimanded by God through Leon's courage to obey God and speak out, and I felt embarrassed and could feel the colour rising in my cheeks. I was immediately led to say 'sorry' to God for my wrong attitude and to surrender back to His ways for my life.

Leon then went on to say, "God also told me to tell you that just like Meshach, Shadrach and Abednego were in the fiery furnace and God was with them, (A Bible story in the book of Daniel, Chapter 3) Grace, you are in the fiery furnace too, but God is with you, and He is going to turn up the heat!"

I knew in that moment that another battle was about to take place in my life. Thankfully, I had no idea what was ahead, but I had every reassurance from God that He was with me every step of the way, so I had nothing to fear.

I found myself praying over my children's lives, that they would be protected from harm, and that whatever was going to happen would not be about them. God honoured that cry of a mother's heart and took me through a continued journey of transformation that would affect my life forever.

You will seek me and find me when you seek me with all your heart.

Jeremiah 29:13

When we surrender our lives to God we can talk to Him and He hears our prayers. But sometimes we can do it out of habit, not relationship. Jesus desires to have an intimate relationship with us, that as we talk to Him we will hear Him, and see His answers come.

How difficult would a marriage be if a husband walked into a room, spoke to his wife about his day, his concerns, his achievements, and difficulties, but, then he turned and walked out of the room without his wife being able to partake in the conversation at all? There would be a complete breakdown of the relationship between them as the husband didn't have time to listen to his wife. He has no concern for her welfare or her anxieties, he doesn't want to listen to the wisdom she may be able to speak into his situations to help him or encourage him.

This is how many people treat God. We talk 'at Him', not 'with Him'. We complain, grumble, stress out and throw everything at Him in attitude, and we make it all about us. Having done so, we then walk away without considering what God might say back to us, how He might want to help us, lead us and show us His answers.

I encourage you to choose to have a relationship with God by seeking Him with all of your heart, and to stay quiet in His presence, so that you will know what He wants to say to you too. Relationship is all about two-way communication.

I call out to the Lord, and he answers me from his holy mountain.

Psalm 3:4

I call on you, my God, for you will answer me;
turn your ear to me and hear my prayer.

Psalm 17:6

God says:

'Call to me and I will answer you and tell you great and unsearchable things you do not know.'

Jeremiah 33:3

God does hear our prayers and he does give us answers. He doesn't always give it immediately or in the way that we would like, but His ways and His timing are always perfect. We pray for what we think we 'want'. God gives us what we 'need'. If there is a delay in the answer being given don't give up hope. It may be that we need to go through a transition time to grow, transform and be prepared to receive the answer that God knows that we need most. Be patient and trust God. His ways are always best.

11

Butterflies and Mystery

Everyday life was becoming more of a challenge. Esther was amazing in her sensitivity to the situation, finding different ways to help me to go out so that I didn't get 'cabin fever' and giving me constant opportunity to talk out how I was feeling so that I could process events day by day and not bottle up my emotions, which would then become buried and cause extra stress to my body. But, because I was so slow in my failing leg strength, it restricted us both for how far we could go.

Esther appeared to be patient in the moment of what we were doing, but she was in fact becoming very frustrated with the limitations that we had. I was privileged to go to the Lake District with them both on a Christian holiday. A large house party of about 85 people. I would stay in the hostel and continue my studies of Christian messages, while everyone else went out for the day on walking expeditions and other activities that I couldn't partake in. Then after the evening meal, I would enjoy social time mixing with everyone and hearing about the events of their day. Due to chronic fatigue that was beginning to become part of my life, I would have to retire early to bed, leaving everyone else to carry on without me.

By this time I was very slow in my walking ability and I used the furniture, or walls or held lightly onto Esther's arm to keep my balance. It was painful to stand and I had to really concentrate on putting one foot in front of the other to maintain my ability to walk. But I was determined not to lose the use of my legs!

People would never say anything directly to me, but after I had gone to bed they would talk openly to Esther about me. They were of the opinion that I would be better off using a wheelchair. When Esther shared their suggestions with me I became upset. I felt betrayed because they couldn't talk openly to me, but could talk about me behind my back. I felt judged, yet they had no idea what I was going through. I found myself isolating away as I felt I couldn't trust anyone. Why does everyone have to have an opinion about other people and what they think they should do, even when they are not interested in knowing the full story? And I felt let down by Esther, who was obviously in agreement with their suggestion of me using a wheelchair, even though she knew my fear of losing the use of my legs. I was thankful when we were able to go home.

In time, I would have to submit to using elbow crutches around the home. Then, on one of our trips to a local indoor shopping centre, I submitted to using a mobility scooter that could be hired for the day. Another friend of Esther's went with us, a lady from Japan, and I found myself following them both at a distance. They were chatting away, sometimes in Japanese, so I had no idea what was being said, even if I had been close enough to hear, which invariably I wasn't.

While they explored inside, I would wait outside the shops that were inaccessible to me with the scooter because of the lack of space. In one such moment I caught sight of my reflection in the plate glass window and I realised how frail and vulnerable I looked, and I fought back the tears.

But then, the truth of Esther's heart was exposed as I followed them both through a large store. She looked back to check and ask if I was okay. I assured her that I was and I commented about the scooter being easier to use than I thought. In a moment, she stopped dead in her tracks, looked at me and just loudly blurted out, "Thank goodness for that. It's a pity that you haven't given in to using one before now!"

Her frustration of the limitations put upon her by my physical frailty over recent months whenever we had gone out together had just bubbled over, and the truth was exposed. I was shocked, saddened and hurt, but I held it together until we got home.

Whenever we had talked about the difficulties, I had been honest with Esther about how I felt and my fear of losing the use of my legs. I had also been concerned about the effect on her and the limitation it caused whenever we went out. But she constantly reassured me that it was okay. She had no problem helping me, in fact, she loved to do so. I made sure that she knew how much I appreciated her help, and I was so thankful for our friendship.

But now, as we had to talk it through, I realised that Esther had not been totally honest about how she felt in the moment of helping me, how frustrated she was at how slow I was walking, holding her back from being able to achieve what she had wanted to do for herself.

Every situation we go through in life affects everybody else around us, often without us realising it. We can all see things through our own perspective, but we do not always consider other people's perspectives. Unless we talk to each other with an open heart, in complete honesty, and without fear of causing upset, then misunderstandings will always take place, someone will always feel abused, let down or not valued. Someone will end up getting hurt.

In this situation, I had been concerned for Esther's welfare too, but I had believed what she had said to reassure me, that it was okay for her to help. But at this moment the truth was exposed, and we had to go back to the drawing board. We also had to talk it out in truth and choose to forgive each other for the hurt caused. We had to try and re-evaluate how we should go forward. Should I continue to live at Esther's house? Was it time to consider using a wheelchair?

As medical tests continued I developed more symptoms, I was having problems with water retention, swallowing, chronic fatigue, and my skin hurt so much that even wearing clothes was painful. My hands and fingers didn't work very well due to the pain and my grip became weak.

One of the medical tests I had to have done was a muscle biopsy. I watched the surgeon make a small incision into the side of my left leg and then use a surgical instrument to remove several samples of muscle from inside my thigh. On completion, I watched her put two stitches in to close up the open wound, apply a see-through plaster over the wound, and then bind my leg tightly with a crepe bandage to prevent my leg from swelling. I was then advised to keep the bandage on tightly for the next 24 hours.

On returning home I found that the bandage had slipped down to my knee. I went to my bedroom to redress it, and as I did so, I noticed through the see-through plaster that the wound had begun to bleed. As I checked it out, I shuddered from head to foot. Touched by the presence of God and His intimacy to me once again, the tears flowed.

Since 2003 God has spoken to me through butterflies, teaching me about my identity in Him, how He sees me. And whenever I need confirmation that I am doing the right thing in my choices, he will get my attention through a butterfly, whether it is real ones flying around, or a picture drawn by a child, or maybe a photograph. He knows how to get my attention and draw me into His will. He knew in this moment how to get my attention. This is how the wound bled:

Blood pools, blood runs, but it doesn't normally make symmetrical shapes like it did in this butterfly!

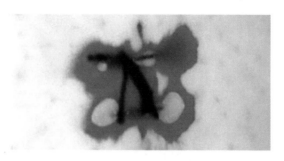

I asked God what He was saying. His answer: "Whatever the outcome of these test results, you are in the mystery of God, I am with you and I am taking you through."

I was about to re-apply the bandage when my younger son Lawrence, who was visiting, came into the room not realising what I was doing. He saw the butterfly on my thigh and in shock he exclaimed, "MUM, Why have you had a tattoo of a butterfly done on your thigh?" I explained what had happened and he was amazed too because it just looked so real. Then we both laughed at the idea of me having a tattoo done. My children had such things, but it just wasn't me!

Three days later, as the wound began to dry out a letter 'H' appeared in the butterfly. In that moment I knew that I was being promised by God that one day my healing would come.

When I went back to see the consultant for the muscle biopsy test results, he was a little edgy as he admitted that he knew my body was in serious distress, that I was in radical pain and I needed help to learn how to live with it, but he didn't know how to go forward with the test results to help with any form of diagnosis. They were mystified and didn't know what else to do to help me.

I smiled and said, 'So I really am in the mystery of God then, aren't I!"

He relaxed, smiled and said, "Yes, because He probably knows more about what is going on in your body than we do."

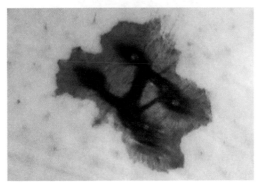

A letter 'H' appeared in the wound as it dried out!

In him we have redemption through his blood, the forgiveness of our trespasses, according to the riches of his grace, ⁸which he lavished upon us, in all wisdom and insight ⁹making known to us the mystery of his will, according to his purpose, which he set forth in Christ ¹⁰ as a plan for the fullness of time...

Ephesians 1:7-10

When Jesus was crucified on the Cross his body was brutally beaten and he bled profusely. In Old Testament days animals were sacrificed at the alter by a Priest. All the mistakes of the people were laid on a goat that was then sent into the desert to die. The people then received forgiveness for what they had done wrong. That's where the saying 'made a scapegoat' comes from.

But God replaced animal sacrifices by allowing His Son Jesus to be nailed to the Cross. He became the ultimate, perfect 'sacrifice' to save our lives and give us a new beginning with God so that our mistakes can be forgiven. This didn't happen because we deserve it, this happened because God is so gracious. He loves us too much to let us go, so His Son Jesus died on our behalf, that we can live a life in relationship with God, no matter what we have done wrong, if we choose to.

His love and grace were 'lavished' upon us, which means they were given generously, extravagantly, without limit! He is willing to give us wisdom and help us to understand situations in a new way, as we see things though His heart and not our own. He reveals the 'mystery' to us to achieve His plans in our lives, through our love for Jesus, that everything comes together for a purpose, in His time plan.

God has a plan. Will you include Him in your life to follow His plans for you? When we say 'yes' to follow Jesus we are giving God permission to show us His plan. If we choose not to include Jesus we remain blinded to God's plan.

What choice are you making?

PART FOUR

SURRENDERED
TO CHANGE

12 | Wheels and Ways

Although what had happened in the breakdown of communication with Esther had been upsetting at the time, it cleared the air between us as we talked it out, I continued to live in their home and we worked together to find the right way forward. It was therefore only a few weeks later when I asked Esther to take me to a disability aid shop so that we could have a look at wheelchairs and consider our options. The pain was mounting, medication was constantly being increased in strength and caused a sense of living in a thick fog, I was slower in my mental co-ordination and awareness of things going on around me. The pain was being suppressed, but not removed, and I was constantly tired with chronic fatigue that became worse with physical exertion.

For so long I had fought not to lose the use of my legs. Each time I went out I had to focus intensely on keeping my balance, willing one leg to move in front of the other with each step that I took. I couldn't converse with Esther because all of my physical and mental energy went into walking. I couldn't look at anything or anyone else around me, as I concentrated so hard on what my body was trying to do.

That day, 9th June 2009, I surrendered my stubborn heartedness to God and asked for His help. I didn't want to give up, I didn't want to give in if things might get better, I didn't want to be accused of doing the wrong thing by buying a wheelchair. I was under the pain management clinic, the chronic fatigue clinic and my local doctor, but nobody had ever suggested that this was what I should do. But I knew I couldn't go on this way.

The salesman was amazing as he helped me consider my choices. I am six feet tall (1.83 metres) and I am not the lightest of people, so I was concerned for anyone who might have to push me in a wheelchair. It had to be made as easy as possible for them too, especially Esther. In a moment a decision was made. What Esther identified as being the "Rolls Royce' of wheelchairs was purchased. It was comfortable for me to sit in, easy for her to push with me in it, and it was lightweight to lift to put in the boot of a car.

Esther was shocked and amazed that we came away with a wheelchair that day. She had thought I would look, go home to think about it and then decide what to do. But I was in the place of knowing I couldn't go any further without receiving this help. After a long battle within myself, not wanting to have to depend on others, not wanting to lose the use of my legs, not wanting to give up my independence, I had finally come to the end of myself and surrendered to what might have to be at that time.

We left the shop and Esther immediately drove to the local seafront area to take me out for a trial run. It was a lovely sunny day with a gentle breeze and as I sat in the chair and she began to push me, I became aware that for the first time in a long time I could relax, look at, and enjoy the scenery and sounds around me. I could hear Esther speaking to me and consider my responses, my body was relaxed and not building up in pain and the overall relief was inexpressible. The immediate relief was phenomenal and in all seriousness, by the end of the walk I could only consider, why had I not done this a long time ago!?

And God is so gracious. Two weeks later I was assessed by a physiotherapist. I didn't feel it was right to use the wheelchair inside the clinic, but as she watched me in my struggles to walk into her assessment room, and completed her examination, she asked how I managed to go out and about. I awkwardly confessed I had just bought a wheelchair, almost expecting her rebuke for doing so. But, she determined that if I had not already bought one for myself, today, she would have sent me home with one from her department. She confirmed there was no other way to go because of the frailty of my body, and I would be causing irreversible damage to myself if I had continued to push through and walk! I was relieved to have her support, and I knew I had been given God's best: my 'Rolls Royce' was far superior to hospital issue.

And so began the next stage of the journey. I could still manage inside the home using elbow crutches and furniture to walk with; the wheelchair was only for use when going out. I didn't want to have to have help from others, but now I had no choice. It was a journey of letting go and letting people into my situation, and as I was pushed around in the chair my life was in their hands...literally!

I had overcome a major physical hurdle in submission to using a chair, but I now entered a new consideration of 'trust', and I had to have a sense of humour to cope. The bottom line is, most people in our lives, including Esther, have never pushed someone in a wheelchair before. They are 'learners' and they definitely needed 'L' plates. It isn't an easy position to be in, sitting in a chair and having no control over the direction you are being taken in, or how the chair will be manoeuvred up and down kerbs or slopes, over cracks and crevices, dips and potholes in the pavement or tipped backwards to cross over thresholds into buildings.

There were many times when it felt like a roller coaster ride at a funfair. Moving quickly forward in one direction and thinking I knew where we were heading, I was often suddenly swung to the right or to the left as something would catch Esther's attention and she veered off to investigate. Or, coming to a sudden halt in a walkway through a clothing store, thinking that Esther was still with me but might be looking at clothing on a rail, I would continue our conversation. Only when approached by a stranger to ask if I was okay did I realise I was sitting alone talking to myself, because Esther had gone between the clothing rails where it was not wheelchair accessible to quickly look at something that had caught her eye, but she had neglected to tell me what she was doing!

As for spacial awareness, well, that was another story. I don't know how many times people nearly finished up on my lap when queueing at a checkout, and Esther would forget that my legs were at least four feet in front of her from where she wanted to stand. Queuing is not one of Esther's favourite pastimes at any time, but ploughing through the opposition in front of us, knocking them down like ten pins in a bowling alley, was not really socially acceptable either!

We attended my son's wedding in Sweden. We travelled together as a family, 17 of us waited for a flight transfer in Stockholm airport. As we all gathered in the waiting area, I was left 'parked' sitting in the wheelchair staring directly at a wall in front of me, while everyone else took a seat and sat chatting together. It took a while to get someone's attention so that I could be turned around to join in!

One of the craziest, scariest moments I ever experienced was when we called in at a superstore shopping complex as we returned from a journey to visit my family in the North East. I had only had the wheelchair for about two weeks. It was Sunday, it was nearly closing time, and Esther wanted to go to the garden centre in a separate building across a massive car park. There was a pedestrian walkway made up of ten interlinking block paved sections that stretched across the car park, and they all had a wooden framed, flower covered tunnelling overhead.

Esther was on a mission: could we get there before it closed? The wheelchair was aimed towards the pathway, and she began to run. Not a good idea I thought. What if we hit a ridge in the paving? I ignored images of seeing myself catapulted head first out of the chair and flying through the air! What if she lost control? Oh dear, a little way off I saw a mother walking towards us with her two young children. Would Esther slow down? Errrrm… no, but the lady saw how fast we were approaching and lovingly took her two children under her outstretched arms, turned them face first towards the side fence like a protective mother hen, and seemingly held her breath as we careered past behind them. I was holding onto the chair arms so tight that my knuckles are white as I called out "Thank you!" to them as we whizzed past. I could see we were approaching the end of the walkway and there was a disability ramp for wheelchairs to gain access to the building. I thought we were heading for it, but no....a sudden swerve to the left took me directly to the five steps at the entrance to the building. The wheelchair came to a sudden halt and Esther said,"You can walk up the steps can't you!"

I am in shock and shaking, then a man who was walking down the disability ramp shouts at Esther in a serious attitude, "Hey, you can't do that to her!" Missing the point completely of what the scenario might have looked like to other people, and without any hesitation, Esther replied, "Yes I can, she can walk the last bit of the way!"

To prevent an angry confrontation taking place I quickly stood up and intervened between them, reassuring the man that I could indeed walk up the steps and that I would be okay. Esther said she thought the ramp was too steep for her to push me up. He said he would have helped her. Again, it was all about different people's perspectives!

Perhaps my next book should be a handbook guide for wheelchair pushers, 'How not to kill your passenger!'

In all seriousness, I will be ever grateful that Esther was prepared to take me out and about using the wheelchair. It was a lot of physical effort to lift it in and out of the car boot and to negotiate different terrains and environments. But it gave a greater freedom to us both on the time we could spend together, and the places we could go to, including attending church. Our conversations of learning together as I shared my continued studies of the Bible were precious, and so many barriers came down between us as we exchanged our childhood and personal growth stories, that would build incredible trust between us for the future.

But it also had its moments of distress with other people's reactions. The first time I was taken to the local supermarket we saw a lady we both knew coming down the aisle towards us. I hadn't seen her for many years, but we all recognised each other and I smiled at her as she approached. Suddenly, she went as far away from me as she could, walking on the other side of the aisle, giving me a wide berth as she went straight past. She then called Esther aside, close to where she was standing, to ask what on earth had happened to me. Although she was encouraged to speak to me directly she didn't feel that she could do so, and abruptly left to continue with her shopping.

This was the first of many times that I would be ignored. One of the first invitations we accepted after getting the chair was to a lunchtime birthday party celebration for a mutual friend. These events had been regular over the years and were one of the few times that we were all able to meet up together for a catch up outside of our church and work commitments. As we entered the restaurant many of my old friends were there from over the years. The stunned silence that settled as we entered set an awkward tone as people struggled to see me in the chair for the first time and didn't know what to say. I tried to carry on as normal, chatting away freely and would have willingly answered any questions, but they didn't want to know. We left early to allow the party to flow freely in a better atmosphere. But I was gutted at their response. Yet again, it is all about perspective. In self-preservation they could not reach out to me, that fear of what they might hear about my situation was too much to bear. That was the last time we would receive any such invitation.

It seemed that because my legs didn't work, people didn't think my brain worked either. We could go to a coffee shop and I could request the order at the counter and give my money to pay. But the waitress would invariably process the payment and then hand any change that was due directly to Esther. It became laughable in the end as I joked about how rich Esther could become at my expense.

But of course, there was a serious side to this journey and things were going to become a lot worse before they would get better, especially with a sudden and difficult decision to have to leave Esther's home in the most dire and unforeseen circumstances.

Trust in the Lord with all your heart and lean not on your own understanding; in all your ways submit to him, and he will make your paths straight.

Proverbs 3:5-6

We have to choose how to trust in any situation or relationship, and things do not always work out how we would like them to, or how we anticipate that they might. But God asks that we surrender to Him in total trust and that we do not work things out in our own logic. That is not always easy because we all have thoughts and a good imagination, we also have desires on how we would like things to happen and we get disappointed when they don't work out how we planned. However, when we choose to trust Him, when we choose to submit to Him, His ways are always best and will take us on the straightest route for our best future. I had to learn how to trust as this story unfolded. I didn't always like God's ways, or what other people did to me, but as I look back on all that has happened I now understand the bigger picture, and I can see how He has ordered my path for my future.

13

Disaster Waiting to Happen

Of all the steps of my journey that I share with you, this chapter is the most difficult to write. As my God given best friend of now 30 years, and someone who is more like a sister to me, I love Esther dearly, and I have no desire to disparage her character or her reputation. However, this is something we walked through together; it is part of the story of God's perfect plan for both of our lives, that only in time to come would we understand as we saw the bigger picture unfold.

Moving into their home with Esther and her husband John was a Godsend in so many ways. We didn't take the decision lightly and only after much conversation and prayer, could we all three submit into agreement of the situation. We knew we shared a vision in Jesus and wanted only the will of God to be fulfilled. For me, it was 'one step' into the next phase of my journey. I had no agenda except to focus on my relationship with Jesus. My time aside with him was important in prayer and learning and whatever else would happen, I would face one day at a time, one moment at a time in total surrender. I had known them for 21 years and Esther was my God given best friend who was more like a sister to me, and our hearts were united in Jesus. God was up to something, we just didn't know what.

Esther is a very different character to me. She was focused on the same vision but her imagination and agenda of how things should happen would give her many expectations that were not fulfilled, and therefore lead to disappointments. Many changes happened in a short space of time. Some of their children came back unexpectedly to live at their parent's home for many months at a time. My own son and his fiancé needed temporary help and came to stay for 4 months too, for which we were all very grateful and valued their love and support. Esther and John were like second parents to my children in many situations of help that were needed over the years.

The home was busy in so many ways. Esther worked part time, her husband full time and very long hours. They undertook many major house renovations during the first twelve months of my stay, so there were builders constantly coming in and out, and it generated a lot of DIY decorating etc to be done by Esther. So having lots of people around that she hadn't anticipated being there was a stressful time for her, and over time I could see it was taking its toll. I helped as much as I could despite my physical frailty but a distance began to build up between us and even conversations in Jesus came to a halt. Then obviously, helping me go to hospital appointments was an added burden of responsibility, but whenever I suggested I would get someone else to help out, Esther was reluctant to let me do so.

The more I tried to help her and speak to her about my concerns, the more she withdrew from me. So things became very tense, as yet again, Esther could not admit the truth of how she was really feeling. Sadly, when she did want to talk anything through she would go to other people and be influenced by their opinions, and that would flood back into the home in many different attitudes.

It all came to a head suddenly, late one October evening in 2010, when having bottled everything up for so long, Esther erupted like a volcano and was unable to be appeased. It culminated in me having to leave her home in the early hours of the morning to go to my son's home for the night. Or that's what I thought. It transpired that our friendship would break down completely, I would not be allowed to move back in, and it would take another five years before full reconciliation would take place!

(Another journey, another book.)

But, God had a plan…

I was to spend the next seven weeks living with Charles, his wife Elaine and their baby son who was only three weeks old when I moved in. They were living in the house that I owned, as they had done so for the last two years. I literally landed in the middle of the night to stay in their spare room that was cluttered up with storage of their possessions. They were not expecting to have visitors! I was raging in pain, physically weak, emotionally wrecked and I didn't know what I was going to do. As it became clear that I could not go back to Esther's home, I had to look for somewhere else to live. This house was not practical for me to live in with my continued physical deterioration, and I had no intention of asking my son and his family to move out.

I moved into my new home seven weeks later, a third floor flat in a privately rented apartment block ten minutes away from my son. Financially, it was a heavy burden to set up and live in my new home, but by God's grace and provision, it all came together. I was still in shock at the outcome of recent events and I was seriously concerned for Esther's welfare, believing that she was having some sort of breakdown, but she withdrew from our friendship in her own emotional pain and I didn't know what to do.

Over the next four weeks, I went through the Christmas period and into the New Year. It was now 2011. Emotionally and physically, I was still reeling from recent events, and I was housebound as nobody knew where I was except my family. All other friends had already withdrawn over the years, and Esther was no longer available to take me out in the wheelchair. Everything within me wanted to curl up, isolate myself away and give up. It affected everything about my life. I would have to find a new church, find new ways to shop and cook for myself again. It was a living nightmare! But I couldn't give up, and the only one I knew I could turn to was Jesus.

There were two churches immediately near to the apartment building where I now live: one across the road and the other immediately next door. But, without help, they might just as well have been ten miles away. I knew where God was showing me to go, the one next door, but I had no way of getting there. It was too far to walk with my elbow crutches and I couldn't use my arms to propel the wheelchair myself. My children were too busy working and I just didn't know what to do.

Ironically, one of Esther's sons and his wife Lorna lived in the same apartment block, directly opposite my flat. Lorna came over one day to see how I was settling into my new home, and asked what I was going to do about Church. I shared my predicament and she graciously offered that on the following Sunday she would push me down to the Church in my wheelchair, leave me there for the service while going to her own Church, and then if needed, she would come back to pick me up again.

By Sunday, I was confident that if I was in the right Church, someone would offer to take me home and Lorna would not have to come back for me. It was daunting going to a new Church, especially as I was by myself once Lorna left, and I was restricted to the wheelchair. But yet again, God is faithful. The welcome I received was so caring and easy, within five minutes two people had already offered to make sure I would get home safely.

The day before going to the new Church I had surrendered everything of myself back to God and His plan for my life. I laid down the vision He had given me in 2003, and said I would not do anything unless He clearly invited me to do so. During the last seven years, I had been totally isolated away listening to Christian teaching, reading books and growing in my faith. In recent weeks I had told Esther that I couldn't seem to absorb anything more. I felt like a dry sponge put into a bowl of water. It soaks and soaks up the water until it is so full that when it is picked up it drips water all over everything. I felt that I had soaked and soaked in Christian teaching and was so full I couldn't absorb anything else. I was ready to 'drip', but I had nowhere to go with what I had.

So, when someone asked on that first visit to the Church whether I did small group Bible Study I was taken aback. I didn't answer the question, I just said that I wouldn't do anything in the Church unless I had a good relationship with the leadership and they knew who I was, and what I was doing. Their response was to say that in their opinion I was someone who was safe to be around, as I had such a great attitude and honour towards the leadership. I was told by that same lady that "I had something that they needed." I didn't know what it was that she saw as she looked at me intensely, but I knew that the only thing that I had, that they needed, was Jesus!

As I had moved to live in a new area of town I also had to change my doctor. I had to join a surgery closer to my home. As I went through their assessment procedures to see if they would accept me onto their register, I eventually had an appointment with one of their doctors. Once he had completed his physical examination and confirmed that I could be a patient, I had a sudden outburst of conversation where I declared to him:

"I am not in denial of my medical condition and I know I need your professional help and support at this time, for which I am very grateful. However, one day, I will walk into this room and no longer need to use a wheelchair. I will be pain-free, totally healed and I will dance!"

Most doctors would have probably looked at me and thought 'We have got a right one here', but not this doctor. He kindly took hold of my hand, looked me in the eye and boldly said, "And on that day, Grace, I will dance with you."

As I declared God's promise that I would one day be healed, the doctor came into agreement with me. That doctor was to become a great support as I continued through a very difficult physical deterioration over time to come. He was also the one who would one day dance with me in my healing.

> [22] let us draw near to God with a sincere heart and with the full assurance that faith brings, having our hearts sprinkled to cleanse us from a guilty conscience and having our bodies washed with pure water. [23] Let us hold unswervingly to the hope we profess, for he who promised is faithful. [24] And let us consider how we may spur one another on toward love and good deeds, [25] not giving up meeting together, as some are in the habit of doing, but encouraging one another—and all the more as you see the Day approaching.
>
> **Hebrews 10:22-25**

Isolated alone in my new home I drew closer to God and continued to grow in faith. The situation I had left behind when moving out of Esther's home was agony, and I found myself constantly running things over and over in my mind, concerned for her welfare, questioning how we ever ended up in this position, talking it through with God, asking forgiveness for anything and everything that I might have done wrong. These were often my own thoughts rather than God showing me anything in particular, but I was anxious for things to be sorted out and I didn't want any wrong on my part to block what God wanted to do.

I know God is faithful, and I knew it was wrong to isolate myself, no matter how I felt, so I couldn't stop going to church. It is so important that we do meet with other people and to encourage each other. Going to church was as much about how I could help others, as well as to help myself, by choosing to move forward with my life.

14

Promises

I continued to deteriorate physically and, within six months of moving into my flat, I became wheelchair dependent indoors as well as out. By God's grace, I was given charitable funding to buy an electric wheelchair with a reclining seat and a headrest to support my failing body in a better way, and to make it easier for me to move around. I couldn't go out alone as I was so disorientated when the chronic fatigue kicked in. But it was easier for people to help as they no longer had to push me around in the original wheelchair unless I had to go somewhere by car.

A few weeks after I began at the Church, a home group came to meet in my home so that I could join in, as it was impracticable for me to go where they used to meet. Within two months, I had fallen into leading the group in Bible study, as their previous leader had stepped aside to do other things. This was only the beginning of how God would open up many opportunities for all that He had taught me in the last seven years to spill out into the lives of other people.

I made many new friends in the Church, especially through the group that I was leading. People were so kind and willing to help out in so many ways according to my different needs. Whether it was escorting me to church meetings, picking up shopping, doing the ironing, washing windows, or other simple domestic chores, people were absolutely amazing in the sacrifice of their time and energy to help.

My daughter, Kaitlin, was a joy to have around when she was able to come and stay between her work responsibilities. Concerned that I should eat a healthy diet, she would do a mass cooking session and portion up meals into the freezer, so that they could be reheated easily in the microwave. I was so spoilt by her attention to detail in variety, balance, and textures, especially because of the swallowing problem that had developed.

Other people would occasionally drop in freshly cooked meals too. Someone else would occasionally go to a greengrocer, rather than a supermarket, to buy the best quality fresh fruit to make a fruit salad. I was so touched by the different ways that everyone thought of to bless me. Dependent on the weather, I was sometimes supported to go out for a short while in the fresh air, just to have a change of scenery.

A trip to the seafront, which was a short walk from my home, feeling the sea breeze blow through my hair, and having the occasional ice-cream, are just some of the memories I will treasure forever. I hadn't known my friend Josie for very long when she suggested that we do this for the first time. I was blessed because she understood some of the concerns when using a wheelchair, as she had previous experience through helping her elderly mother. I was using my electric wheelchair, so she didn't have to push me, but her awareness of the hazards around me, and sensitivity as we crossed the road, and mingled through crowds of people was amazing, and I felt incredibly safe.

On that occasion, we enjoyed a hot chocolate together as it was a little breezy outside. As we were about to leave the café and walk home, it suddenly began to rain. I didn't have an umbrella or a blanket with me, and Josie knew, that while sitting in the wheelchair, my clothing would absorb moisture very quickly, and I would then feel cold. Without hesitation, she went to the lady behind the counter and came back to me, holding a small pile of plastic carrier bags. In a moment, my legs and body were duly covered with blue and white striped plastic, to protect me from the rain! It brought a whole new meaning to the phrase 'bag lady'!

I was a little embarrassed, but also bemused by her ingenuity. As we walked home, I couldn't help but laugh inwardly at the image I must have been presenting to anyone walking by. But, it worked amazingly well, and I was thankful. As we approached my home I couldn't help but see the funny side as I asked the question, "Does my bottom look big in this?" It was a great ice breaker between new friends, and I am so thankful for all that Josie has been in my life, and in so many different ways since.

I really appreciated and valued all the help that God was providing, but it was a whole new journey of influence from other people too. The familiarity of relationship with Esther had been so different; she knew me so well and, until the breakdown, we had flowed together so easily. Now I found myself at the mercy of lots of people's good ideas and what they thought that I needed as they tried to protect me. I constantly had my free choice taken away from me, especially when they didn't let me know about some of the events that were going on around me, because they decided that I was just 'too frail' or 'too ill' to consider going, because of what they thought they saw in my situation.

That was the point that I had to learn to stand up in my true identity. I wasn't in denial of my medical condition, but I had to determine, understand, and know for myself that the wheelchair was not my identity! Wherever I went, that was all people could see – my wheelchair. I was often ignored as people talked over my head as though I couldn't hear them. I was avoided by many people at all cost, as though I had the plague and was too dangerous to be around, and many conversations came to an abrupt halt as I came nearby as people seemed uncomfortable by what they saw.

You would think that two wheelchair users coming face to face in a store would be able to say 'hello' to each other, but as I chose to do so, the other person would invariably drop their head, as though in shame, and they would not respond to me. After a while, I realised that they were so crushed and broken in spirit, they seemed to have lost their identity, and they didn't expect anyone to notice them, let alone speak to them.

It became a wake-up call for me in my own circumstances. I didn't want to lose myself or my identity. I realised that I had to stand up for who I was and for what I could still do. Where there was loss of ability I had to find a new way to do things, or accept my limitations. I had to let go of who I thought that I was, and in it all, adjust to my new life now. Our circumstances are not our identity unless that is what we submit to.

In every situation of life, we have choices. Our choices affect ourselves and often other people, and other people's choices affect us, sometimes in good ways, but also in bad. As people began to make choices for me, they didn't realise that they were making me a 'victim' of my circumstances. They were limiting me in their mindset of what they thought my life was like, and what they thought that I should or shouldn't do. They were lovely, precious people who were doing it with every good intention to love me as I was, and to protect me from harm, and I love every one of them dearly, but I knew I had to hold onto who I really was, and nobody else could do that for me.

I knew that in 2009, through the butterfly pictures that bled on my leg, God had promised me that one day my healing would come. And I used to constantly speak that out to people. I used to boldly declare:

"I know that one day Jesus is going to heal me, and even if it is in death that I get my perfect body, God has still kept His promise!"

It is so important what we choose to believe, and how we speak about ourselves and our circumstances. Our words have power. In the Bible it says our words 'speak life or death, curse or blessing'. In every medical investigation that I had, a medical prognosis was given out of what the doctors believed my life would be like, because of the probabilities they have seen in other people of similar conditions.

At the Pain Management clinic I was advised that there was no cure for my chronic pain, so they would have to teach me how to live with this chronic pain condition for the rest of my life, keeping me balanced on medication that would increase in strength over time.

The Chronic Fatigue clinic told me the same thing. There was no cure, they could only help me learn how to live with it, and handle it on a day to day basis.

In time to come, the physical frailty would eventually go to my vocal chords and I would lose the sound of my voice completely. The Voice Therapist advised she was to help me to learn how to communicate without a voice for the rest of my life!

But I knew what God had promised, and as each prognosis was given I used to pray in my head as they spoke out their negative words, and I used to believe in the promises of Jesus. As I had focused on my faith journey over the years of being so ill, I had come to understand in a deeper way about the power of the Cross, and I chose to believe for that power to be released over my life.

Then, on 30th April 2011, God spoke clearly to me through a story in the Bible where Jesus raises a dead man back to life. When Jesus receives the message that Lazarus is sick, Jesus replies, "This sickness will not end in death." In that moment I just knew that God was saying that I would be healed in this lifetime, this sickness would not be the death of me, and the glory would go to Jesus. He also showed me that the delayed answer was gaining interest and that He would heal others through my life while I was in the difficulties.

So my declaration changed. From now on I would confidently declare; "I know that one day Jesus is going to heal me!"

11 Now a man named Lazarus was sick. He was from Bethany, the village of Mary and her sister Martha. ² (This Mary, whose brother Lazarus now lay sick, was the same one who poured perfume on the Lord and wiped his feet with her hair.) ³ So the sisters sent word to Jesus, "Lord, the one you love is sick."

> **When he heard this, Jesus said, "This sickness will not end in death. No, it is for God's glory so that God's Son may be glorified through it."**
>
> **John 11:1-4**

> **But he was pierced for our transgressions, he was crushed for our iniquities; the punishment that brought us peace was on him, and by his wounds we are healed.**
>
> **Isaiah 53:5**

When crucified on the Cross, Jesus suffered mercilessly at the hands of his killers. He was pierced with nails in His hands and feet, by a sword into His side. He suffered every emotion we can ever go through. He suffered so that we could be forgiven our mistakes and live in peace despite them. He was wounded physically and emotionally in ways that we may never experience or comprehend, so He empathises with us in our hurts and emotions. He understands how we feel! He carried all our sicknesses and diseases on himself.

Then, He was raised from the dead three days later and completed the victory over all things, including death! By faith in Him, we walk in that same victory and freedom. We receive our healing because of what Jesus has already done at the Cross. He did this for me. He did this for you!

PART FIVE

FAITH IN FRAILTY

15

Determination and Stubbornness

There came a point in 2011 where I could not cope with my own personal care. I could shower myself, but then chronic fatigue would take over and I would struggle to get dried and dressed. This was just before I began to use an electric wheelchair indoors, so I was still attempting to walk around using elbow crutches, the furniture or the walls to keep my balance. When you are shy, insecure and a very private person it is not easy to consider that someone else should be allowed to help you in such things.

But honesty is always the best way forward. Only when we can admit that we have a problem can a solution be sorted out.

My friend Joan could see that I was very fatigued, and she asked me how I was coping. In a casual conversation, I happened to say that I found completing my morning routine through the shower more of a struggle these days. Then, as we talked in general, the subject was dropped, but it wasn't to be forgotten.

A few days later, Joan kindly offered help every morning to enable me to have a shower. I was shocked, I felt awkward and embarrassed, and everything within me wanted to say "No." But, why do we do that? Why, when it was so obviously a simple answer to the problem, did I want to resist!? I made excuses. I focused on how time-consuming it would be for her. I couldn't possibly expect her to make such a commitment.

However, she wasn't the only one willing to help. Linda, another lady in the Church had already expressed her concerns about me to Joan and had wondered what she could do to help me. They had agreed between them that if I was willing, they were prepared to do alternate mornings between them so that every day was covered. I had no excuses. I was humbled by their willingness to help me, but I was the one who had to have the grace to receive what they wanted to do for me. I was so thankful for the answer to a serious problem that I was dealing with, but everything in me was screaming, "I do not want to have to do this!"

I prayed so hard that first morning for God's help to enable me to accept what Joan was going to do. I felt extremely awkward, I didn't want to be exposed in front of anyone else! But, I had nothing to fear. Joan was incredibly compassionate, understanding and sensitive in her approach. As we talked through the practicalities we came to an agreement: I would shower myself, wrap myself in a towel and sit down, then Joan would dry what I couldn't manage to do and dress me in a way that protected my dignity. And that's exactly what we did. I had truly been given God's best!

I duly showered and did all I could manage, but as fatigue began to creep over me I sat down, wrapped in a towel, waiting for help. Joan carefully helped dry me and dressed my upper body with such tender care, love and protection. Then she knelt in front of me with a towel in her hands and went to dry my feet. As she took my foot in her hand I was suddenly overcome with uncontrollable sobbing and emotion. In that moment I saw Jesus. He was kneeling in front of me tending to my feet, just as He had washed his disciple's feet before the last supper, as explained in the Bible. (John 13:1-17)

I was broken, brought to the end of myself to receive the help that God provided, not just in this moment, but for what was to come in the future. Poor Joan was initially mortified at my response, as knowing how much pain I was in, she thought she had hurt me as she had handled my foot. I gave her every reassurance and shared what I had just experienced through her grace to help me. We were both released to relax, work together, and enjoy our morning conversations together in Jesus whenever she came through the door.

Linda and Joan faithfully came to help me every day and I adjusted to accept what was needed. But there came a time when I knew that they could not support me like this forever. I, therefore, made a big decision and contacted Social Services to ask them for their help. I realised that my family had to be allowed to be family, my friends allowed to enjoy our friendship, and nobody should carry any responsibility for me in my frailty, except for momentary need when with me.

Our time together could then be quality time and not just practical need. Professional services could then support in every other way. This was a major decision that I did not take lightly. I was giving up more and more of my independence as the situation deteriorated over time.

So, from July 2011, I had to submit to having professional carers come into my home, four times a day to help me with bathroom needs and provision of food. It is daunting to have so many strangers come into your home to help you, and learning how to make their job easier for them as they are not familiar with who you are. It can be difficult to find a way to have your own needs met, in the individuality of your situation, and not just by what they might do for other people.

It was also a time of submission without giving up. Just as 'giving in' to having a wheelchair was one part of my journey of learning to accept help, this was another. For the first few days, they observed what I could and could not do, so that they were able to determine the best way to help me.

I would spend a lot of my time in a riser/recliner chair to rest my body. To go to the bathroom I would raise the chair to help me to stand up, then walk while holding onto the chair, and then the walls, to cover the four metres to the bathroom door. I would inevitably manage to get half way and then my body would surge in agonising pain, weakening my legs. I would stop for a while, with the palms of my hands against the wall and desperately pray that my legs would not give way. Only when feeling strong enough to do so, would I then continue to the bathroom.

Mary, one of the carers, observed me doing this for three days and then said, "I really admire your determination to be independent and to continue to do as much for yourself as you can. But can I advise that there is a fine line between 'stubbornness' and 'determination'!" This lady was a 'truth teller', and we all need them in our lives. The truth hurt, but it was being said for my own good, and I knew it. She then continued to explain that, "The first half of the walk to your bathroom is your determination and you are able. But from the point that you stand still, hoping that your legs will not give way, and then you choose to continue to walk, that is sheer stubbornness! We are here to help you. After going as far as you can go, we could then use a glider chair (a small steel-framed chair on wheels) to push you the rest of the way so you do not stress and hurt your body."

It all made sense, but to accept that my walking ability was in further decline was a hard truth to face. However, the carer was right, and I reluctantly allowed them to use a glider chair to take me from the lounge to the bathroom. But as my body became weaker I had to reassess what I was doing, and within weeks I was to have a smaller electric wheelchair for use indoors.

I met many different ladies as they came in their professional capacity through my door. Not all of them came with the right attitude, but as I got to know them I had to remember that they do a very demanding, difficult job, and some of the people they encounter are not always appreciative of what they were doing for them, and could often be quite abusive. I would, therefore, affirm them for the positive things that they did for me, and they would soften in their demeanour towards me. We all need encouragement.

This whole situation wasn't just about me. I was ever mindful and thankful to everyone for all the help that I received. I praised God for helping me endure through it all. Over time, I began to realise that I had been given a whole new opportunity to help other people through all that I had learned in my studies over the years. I didn't hide the fact that I was a Christian, but I didn't force my belief onto people either.

I would listen as people shared their innermost fears, hurts and concerns in general conversation as they helped me. I would then speak the wisdom given from God to help them understand the choices that they had, and encouraged them how to look at their situation from a different perspective. I would explain something that I had learned - that if we keep doing the same thing over and over, nothing will ever change. To have something different, we have to be prepared to do something different!

I cannot count how many long conversations took place as I entered the bathroom. I would spend a lot of time sitting on the toilet, all dignity protected, and answer questions that naturally came up in conversation. But it didn't matter. This was their moment of need and that is where God would meet them, just as He does with everyone, when and where we least expect it. I saw many people's lives move forward in a better way as they contemplated their choices and took action to resolve situations instead of just accepting or fighting them.

In time, I was blessed to have two wonderful ladies become my main carers on a full-time basis. Lydia and Monica would visit rotationally every day and over the next five years, they would become very much a part of my extended family. God's provision is always perfect. He always provides the best.

I was always given the best in all circumstances, even if I did resist for a while and struggle to accept what God wanted to do for me. But I got there in the end.

Something I learned very quickly: There is a big difference between 'sympathy' and 'compassion.'

When we sympathise with someone, we have feelings of pity and sorrow for them as they go through some kind of misfortune. Sympathy leaves people in a mess without hope.

When we have compassion, we have feelings of pity and sorrow for people as they go through some kind of misfortune, but we look for ways to help them. We are sensitive to their needs and we go out of our way to encourage them that things will not stay the same forever. We journey with them in some small way to help them see above the circumstances and not be buried under them. Compassion encourages people to look beyond the pain to believe for something better to come.

I didn't have any answers for people in their different needs, but Jesus did. I was privileged to be part of their journey, despite my own difficulties.

As a father has compassion on his children, so the Lord has compassion on those who fear him;
Psalm 103:13

16

Falling Into...

For the first seven years after the road accident, I was drawn into a deeper level of faith as I focused on making time for God. He gave me such a depth and new understanding of who He is, and who He wants to be to each one of us. For every changing moment in this journey, He had answers that I needed, not least when I had to move home yet again.

For many months I had listened to the 'crash, bang, wallop' of major renovations that the owner was making to the flat above mine after the previous tenant had moved out. I had no intention of moving, although I was finding the bathroom in my current flat difficult to use because of limited space, and the shower was over the bath, so I was having difficulty climbing over the bath side to use it. But God had another plan.

I answered a knock at the door to someone in a hurry. They had sprung a leak while doing the plumbing in the bathroom and there was concern that it might leak to my flat too. A bucket was thrust into my hands in case it was needed, and Jack ran to find the caretaker to check the structural setup for where the water was leaking to. He would then come back to see me.

I didn't have a leak and all was quickly sorted. As Jack introduced himself as the landlord of the property above mine, and apologised for the inconvenience of the noise and possible leaks, I found myself asking if I could have a peek at the finished works before the property was let out to a future tenant. I was just being nosey. His wife came to see me two days later with flowers to apologise for the inconvenience of the noise and the leak. We connected easily in conversation as I thanked her for her thoughtfulness.

Two weeks later, escorted in the wheelchair by my friend Josie, I popped up to have a look. The flat was immaculate with all new wooden floors, a new fitted kitchen, and bathroom, and decorated throughout in gentle creams and white. As I peeked into the bathroom, Jack's wife Victoria was just putting the finishing touches to the wall tiles. I told them that whoever moved into the flat would be incredibly blessed as they had done such a great job in the refurbishment. The atmosphere was amazing.

Jack then asked, "Would you consider moving into this flat?" I was stunned as I didn't intend to move. Then as I looked around the bathroom I could see there was a shower over the bath, so I explained that it wasn't suitable for my needs. Without hesitation, Jack immediately advised that if that was the only thing stopping me from taking the flat, he would have the plumber remove the new bath and fit a shower cubicle instead. He would really like to have me as his tenant.

I was amazed that he would be prepared to do such a thing, especially because of the added cost beyond the thousands he had spent on the flat so far. I asked for time to pray about it. I only had until Monday as the letting agent was setting up appointments for viewings from that day. Josie couldn't understand why I didn't say 'Yes' immediately to the offer I had received. In her words, "It was a no brainier." But I needed to know that this was part of God's plan for me.

God is faithful, and as I prayed over the weekend and read my Bible, He clearly showed me that I was being invited by Him to 'go to the other side'. For myself, it was to the flat above – on the other side of my ceiling, and I had nothing to fear. It wasn't that I was afraid, I just didn't want to step out of God's plan for my life!

Jesus calms the storm

That day when evening came, he said to his disciples, **'Let us go over to the other side**.'³⁶ Leaving the crowd behind, they took him along, just as he was, in the boat. There were also other boats with him. ³⁷ A furious squall came up, and the waves broke over the boat, so that it was nearly swamped. ³⁸ Jesus was in the stern, sleeping on a cushion. The disciples woke him and said to him, 'Teacher, don't you care if we drown?'

³⁹ He got up, rebuked the wind and said to the waves, 'Quiet! **Be still!**' Then the wind died down and it was completely calm.

⁴⁰ He said to his disciples, **'Why are you so afraid? Do you still have no faith?'**

Mark 4:35-39

I called Jack on Sunday afternoon and accepted his offer. He was elated, so much so that first thing on Monday morning he brought booklets so that I could choose a shower cubicle, and the plumber had already begun to remove the brand new bath. It was agreed that perhaps I might contribute to the cost of the cubicle as it was a replacement for the new bath. I willingly agreed. I thought it was only fair after all Jack was prepared to alter on my behalf.

I was helped by Josie to go to a nearby plumber's merchant to look at shower cubicles, and after a crazy encounter with a kind hearted shop manager, who it transpired, also believed in Jesus, I purchased a shower cubicle that was ex-display and a new base tray, £1700 in value, for only £600. Yet again, God was my provider and was confirming that He was leading me into this move. All renovations were completed really quickly and a completely new revamp of the layout of the bathroom was made to create as much space as possible. And God continued to show His perfect provision when the cubicle delivered was not the ex-display one that I had chosen to accept at a reduced price; it was a brand new boxed set from stock. Yet again I had been given the best!

On the day I moved into my new home, enabled by the help of many precious people, I duly offered to pay for the shower cubicle as previously discussed, but my offer was rejected, despite my protests. Jack and Victoria were landlords from heaven and over time we were soon to become very good friends. It didn't matter how my needs changed, Jack would do whatever he could to adjust things in the flat to make life as easy as possible for me.

As I settled into my new home I fell into new responsibilities too. Despite my physical frailties, I was already doing two Bible study groups in my home, and now I found a steady stream of visitors continued to come on a regular basis for help in many different situations. All I had to do was offer a listening ear as people chose to talk through their problems, to be a sounding board as they evaluated how they felt about things.

Then the wisdom that God had taught me over the years began to spill out into the situation, to encourage and lead them into the choices that they could take. I saw God answer so many prayers as people were healed physically, emotionally and spiritually. Many would begin a relationship with God for the first time; some who had faltered in their journey wanted to begin again; others were baptised or discipled to understand the Bible in a better way, and then mentored in how to apply what they were learning into their lives. God is amazing, and I was so humbled to be a part of their journey, and so blessed to see people claim freedom from their troubles.

The deterioration in my physicality was debilitating in many ways, but whenever I fell into being there for other people in their moment of need, I was enabled to listen and then to respond appropriately for as long as was required, even if I had to recline out flat on my recliner chair, or appear that I might be asleep as the fatigue affected my muscles and I couldn't open my eyes. I encouraged people that I could still hear what they were saying, and God was my enabler in all things. But outside of those moments, I was so incredibly frail and weak.

Stepping into all that God was asking me to do took me far beyond my comfort zone. I didn't see myself as a leader, but suddenly, people wanted to know what I thought about many things, and would choose to take on board what I spoke through wisdom I had been given by God over the years, and as I watched them apply it to their lives, the transformation in many individuals was profound.

I was humbled by God's grace and how He was teaching me through the circumstance. By the power of His Spirit working in me, I was equipped and enabled to help others understand and receive the love of Jesus. I learned to step into every moment trusting for His will to be done. It was all about Jesus, not about me. People needed Jesus, they didn't need me. I used to make it very clear to everyone that Jesus was the centre of our relationship. He was the only one who could help them. They could trust Him, not me.

One evening as I contemplated what it was all about, as I did many times, God showed me to look at my diary and to see the impact He was having over my life, and through my life. I was led to count the number of visitors I had seen each week, and I was humbled, shocked and amazed to realise that in one year, I had over 2800 visits through my door (Not 2800 people...but visits). With carers, people who came to weekly Bible Study Groups, medical professionals, and the individuals who came to be helped in their difficulties, the visits mounted up. Many came to visit numerous times, and in every conversation, Jesus was the centre as I confessed my faith journey and my healing promise from God.

The carers, Lydia and Monica, continued to help me day by day and met many of my visitors, but as I deteriorated physically they were concerned for my future. Yet, they were witnessing the power and provision of God in my life and they too were excited about my journey.

Some people said they couldn't pray for me anymore, because they had prayed for so long to see me fully recover, and all they could see was that I was getting worse. I had to encourage them to keep praying, as we might be just one prayer short of the breakthrough! But they should also change the attitude of their prayers. I asked them to stop focusing on what they desired to see, my complete recovery and healing, and to believe by faith that one day it would happen. But in the meantime, they should keep praying that God would help me in my everyday situation to endure everything in His grace and continued help and provision.

Human nature desires something specific to happen in every situation; we have expectations of what we want to see or have, and when those expectations are not met, we become disappointed. But it is OUR expectations that SET US UP for disappointment. If only we could hold things more lightly and be open minded to enjoy whatever does happen, we would be so much happier.

So often we tell God what we want Him to do, what we want to see, but we don't allow Him to do things His way, trusting He has it all in hand. His timing and His ways are always perfect.

We do the same with people too, and when they don't comply with our expectations the disappointments kick in, to separate and destroy marriages, friendships, and many other precious relationships, all because we set ourselves up to be disappointed by our own expectations without factoring in other people's choices and ideas too.

"For my thoughts are not your thoughts,
neither are your ways my ways,"
declares the Lord.

Isaiah 55:8

God does not think like we do, or do things our way. He is not bound by time – we can be very impatient; we want everything 'yesterday'. He has a time for everything, an order of events that help us to cope with what He is doing. He is outside the realms of our humanity, physically and emotionally. His power is made 'perfect in our weaknesses'. If we could do it ourselves, we would not need God!

Our God is in heaven; he does whatever pleases him
Psalm 115:3

God was doing as He pleased in my life and I was overwhelmed in so many ways. The constant losses I encountered over the years had been painful; losing my job, moving home four times, friends that had moved on, losing the use of my legs and every other physical frailty that I encountered, all changed my perspective on the meaning of my life.

But every loss was counterbalanced by the love of God that I knew, His faithfulness as He provided for all of my needs, the depth and knowledge that I was taken to in order to learn more about His ways, how He enabled me to cope with every difficulty in my own life, and equipped me to encourage other people in theirs. It was all so amazing and I was so thankful. My hope and my future were both in His hands, and I was learning to let go and to trust Him with every aspect of my life.

17

Stripped

In August 2014 a new frailty came over my body. The muscle weakness affected my vocal chords and I completely lost the sound of my voice. The prognosis was given that it was irreversible. I would never speak again. A voice coach was therefore brought in to teach me how to communicate without a voice. I had the quietest of whisper sounds as I spoke, so quiet that people had to put their ear to my mouth to try to catch anything I tried to say. Inside the home, I used a head microphone to speak into a mini amplifier clipped on my waist; it amplified my whisper, but it wasn't always able to be understood by the hearer, and it was useless in any other environment. I also used voice text on my iPad to type out what I wanted to say, and it would speak my words for me.

Again, I refused to accept the prognosis. I couldn't deny what was happening, but I stood on God's promise that one day He would heal me....and God cannot lie.

This latest development affected a lot of people. Not only could I now not speak, but I became really weak and even more fatigued. I had become housebound through using my wheelchair, as I could only leave my home if I was escorted by someone else, but, up until this point, people visited on a regular basis and I had used the telephone to keep in touch with the outside world.

But now, people stopped visiting because they knew communication was so difficult without a voice. I couldn't use a telephone anymore because they couldn't hear me speak. The isolation that I suddenly found myself in was totally contradictory to the character that I had become. I loved being around people, but yet again, I was being stripped. Except for a couple of close friends, the carers were the only people who came through my door every day, but even they would often find me almost comatose in my chair through increased pain and fatigue. It made their job even more difficult as they sought out new ways to help me.

Barely able to focus on anything because the pain was so distracting and the fatigue was so debilitating, I would play Christian music and just rest in the presence of God. This was something I had surrendered to do repeatedly throughout the years of this ordeal. I would pray to ask for His help, but I would also praise Him, so thankful that I wasn't alone, and I knew that He would help me to cope.

The shortest verse in the Bible is John chapter 11, verse 35. It simply says, "Jesus wept". I knew that in my frailty, in my tears of desperation and my heart crying out to God, that Jesus heard my prayers, He understood how I felt, and He would cry with me and for me, just as He had done so many times in the last eleven years. His love knows no limits, His empathy draws near and He is in the moment with me. He understands. After everything that He endured during His crucifixion there was nothing that He did not understand. His compassion would carry me through and I knew my victory would be through Him.

This is a rare photograph taken of me when I was out at Church in my electric wheelchair. I am in pain and chronic fatigue, unable to open my eyes to interact with people around me.

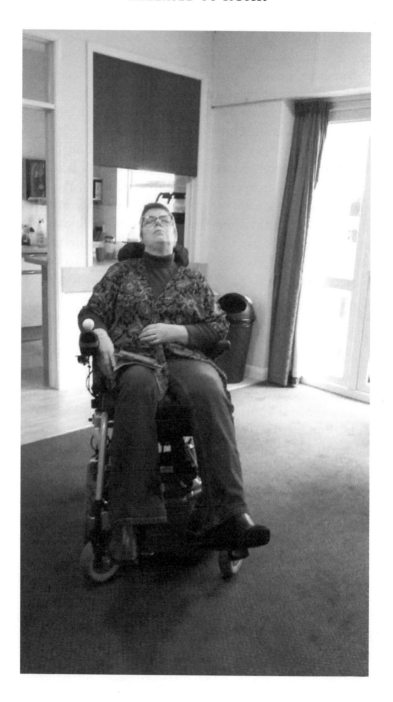

I was so thankful for all that I had been blessed with over the years, but it had also been painful in so many ways, not least the loss of relationship with my best friend Esther. Twenty-three years is a long time to know somebody, and then to lose their friendship. We had journeyed through so much together, our families had grown up together, we had grown in our faith in Jesus together, and we knew we had a future together to help others in their faith journey too.

However, as anger and human disruption had cut into everything that had happened when I was living in her home, the separation was allowed to happen. For myself, it was to be a journey of incredible release into God's plan for my life, to grow into my true identity as a Bible teacher, mentor, and encourager to others, and I am so thankful to God for all that He did for me, and through my life, despite the circumstances.

But all the while, as His plans opened up over my life in such joy and freedom, the negative undercurrent of the unreconciled friendship with Esther ate into me and I ached for resolution to come quickly. I always believed, and I constantly declared that "One day God will reconcile this friendship." But I also knew that God needed two willing hearts to work with. Two hearts to want the same thing. Two hearts to surrender for that reconciliation to happen!

It took five years for that surrender to come, but God's timing is always perfect!

Three times during the five years we had connected in attempts to reconcile, but it had never worked out; in fact, it only made things worse. Then in July 2015, I received an email from Esther advising that the friendship was over. She was moving on with her life and it didn't include me. I was heartbroken. I knew it wasn't right, but Esther had a free will choice. Her choice was impacting my life, giving me no choice, but there was nothing I could do about it, except pray.

Only God could work this out and I only wanted what He wanted. I asked God to enable me to keep my heart soft towards Esther - no anger, no bitterness, no resentment - so that when He did what only He could do, my heart would be pliable in His hands to receive what He wanted to give back, if anything, of our friendship. I knew if I hardened my heart I would block His plans for us.

But so many people do just that; they harden their hearts in their choices, in their pain, in their brokenness and they become resistant to what is best for them in difficult situations. As rejection, anger, and bitterness set in through wrong choices, we become resistant to the possibility of reconciliation in broken relationships, we lose hope of a turnaround in any situation that separates and divides. Our choices affect our lives, but they impact other people's lives too, and not always for the best.

So I was shocked to suddenly receive an email from Esther on my birthday five months later. If I am honest, I felt physically sick when I saw her name come up on my emails. What was she now saying? It was a simple birthday greeting, but she also asked if I would consider meeting with her, even if it was only one more time, as she had to share something with me.

It took me three days to consider and pray about the request. I so wanted to see her, and I had believed nothing was impossible for God to reconcile us. But the memory of the pain from our last three attempts to connect made me cautious, and I didn't want to go through that again. Then I remembered, I had asked God to keep my heart soft to receive whatever He wanted to do in our friendship, so I accepted her invitation to meet up, asking her to come to my home as I was unable to go out.

On January 9th, 2015 Esther came back into my life. It was a shock for her to see how frail I had become, especially as I had no voice. After initial politenesses, she went straight into the reason why she had wanted to meet. After sending the email to bring closure on our friendship back in July, she had become restless within herself; something wasn't right, but she didn't know what. But then, God began to show her various aspects of the journey that we had encountered together, not least, the breakdown that had happened in her home, a breakdown that Esther had consistently blamed me for. In her eyes, it was always 'all my fault!'

There are always two sides to any story, and we are prone to be blind to any other understanding of a situation than the one we choose to believe for ourselves. Now, Esther was having to confront new truths as God showed her different aspects of her own behaviour that had contributed so strongly to the events of that time: How her choices had affected so many other people, how her own actions had caused a lot of distress, how, in her reactions, she had been so wrong. Esther had been brought to her knees, as she had to face the truth, that it wasn't all 'just my fault.'

There were rights and wrongs on both sides, as there always is in a relationship breakdown. But Esther was explaining that she could now understand why some things had happened, in a way that she had not been able to see before. As she then apologised for her own actions that had caused so much trouble, I was asked if I would forgive her. In that moment, as she spoke out the apology, the tension between us broke. I told her that I forgave her, and the dividing wall that had been between us for the last five years immediately came tumbling down. I apologised for the hurt that I had caused her too. As she forgave me, we settled into a conversation of ease between two friends who were comfortable with each other again.

Esther knew that she had to come back and apologise to me, but as five years had gone by, and I had a new life with new friends that she wasn't part of, she believed I would thank her for the apology and ask her to leave. That was always furthest from my heart, as I had always desired and believed for God to reconcile us. But God had also answered my heart's cry, He had enabled me to keep my heart soft to receive what He wanted to give back in our friendship, and I was overjoyed.

Over the next few weeks, we either saw each other or talked on the phone every day, which was a miracle, because Esther could work out what I was saying on the telephone when everybody else found it so difficult. We discussed many things, looking at them from both perspectives as God brought back memories from the agony of the past. As we took responsibility for our actions, apologised and forgave each other, the freedom came very quickly to enjoy our friendship and to trust each other again. Now, after being fully reconciled through God's love and grace, it is just as though the five-year separation never happened. However, we can both see what God did in both of our lives through the circumstances, and our friendship is now stronger than ever.

Over the rest of the year, I became really ill and weak. I wasn't able to go out of my home very often. And eventually, even going to Church was difficult. I had to step aside from leading one of the Bible study groups that I had held in the church, but the group that I was still leading in my home continued coming through my door on a Monday night. I was somehow able to continue to lead using my microphone, and together we shared so much in Jesus. Esther joined us and was accepted for who she was, and when I couldn't do what I needed to do, she would do it for me. We are such different characters, but we complement each other, especially whenever we stand together in Jesus.

I can do all this through him who gives me strength.
Philippians 4:13

It took great courage for Esther to choose to come back through my door, to admit the error of her way, and to want to reconcile. Without Jesus, in our lives, I know that it would never have happened. Pride and denial would have held us both in a prison, especially after so long apart, but grace brought us back together! Individually and together, we had learned so much through the difficulties, and we knew and believed for the best that was yet to come, despite all things.

PART SIX

I Believe In Miracles

18

Invitation

Every day is a new day. As we wake up we are so blessed to be able to breathe, to have life. We have so much to be thankful for regardless of our circumstances. Every morning I would say "Good morning Lord," to God, even though it came out in the quietest whisper. Each day was a day of new possibilities and, after the carer had helped me to shower and dress, I would love to focus on a time of prayer and reading my Bible. To begin the day with God was so important, to include Him in everything, to be thankful for all the good things that I was blessed with, and to surrender everything else that wasn't as I would like it to be, into His hands. He had answers that I needed and I trusted Him.

There were some days when I was so frail I had to wait until my body could cope with reading the Bible, but I could always play worship songs and pray as I waited for my body strength to improve. God was still there, listening, and He knew more about everything that was happening than I did, as He sees the end from the beginning in all things.

As I woke up on Tuesday 6th October 2015 it was one of those days that I had suffered so many times, when this routine would be disrupted. I was so ill I could barely cope with life. The pain and fatigue were unbearable, I hurt so much, even to breathe, and as I lay flat on my recliner chair

I just let the tears roll. I hadn't been very good over the previous few days, so Esther had helped to lead the Bible study group the night before.

Today, Esther was coming over for our weekly prayer time together. When she arrived it was immediately clear to her that I was in a bad way. I had been in this situation many times with other people over the years, and they usually decided to leave, as there was nothing they could do for me, and it was too distressing for them to be around me. I was waiting for Esther to do the same, but she didn't.

The previous evening I had asked Esther to lead the group in taking Holy Communion, something that Christians do to remember what Jesus did for them when He died on the Cross. Today, she brought a booklet with her that she had used to prepare her notes for the evening. As I lay in front of her, not able to open my eyes because of the fatigue in my muscles, it was obvious to Esther that I was too frail to do anything. So, as the booklet was only small, she asked if she could read it to me as I rested.

I have to be honest, all I could think to myself was, 'You can do whatever you want Esther, I really don't care'. This was so unlike me. I loved our prayer times together and I was disappointed not to be able to respond in a more positive way. But Esther was unphased by the situation and quietly, but boldly, began to read the book aloud to me.

The book is called 'Health And Wholeness Through The Holy Communion' and was written by Joseph Prince, the senior Pastor of a Church in Singapore.

As Esther read each page something began to stir in me. I knew that God was speaking to me. The clarity of understanding that came to me about Holy Communion was profound and so powerful, and as she finished the book I knew I had received an invitation from God.

I brought myself back up to a sitting position on the recliner chair so that I could face Esther, and simply said:

"I know, that I know, that I know, that God is asking me to take Holy Communion three times a day, for the next forty days, and He will take me off the medication."

Esther just stared back at me in disbelief and asked, "Where on earth did you get that idea from?" I didn't read anything like that. I couldn't remember what she had read, but I knew that I had heard God. It didn't make sense, it wasn't logical, but I didn't care. I just knew that I knew!

I had been taking pain relief medication for the last twelve years, progressively varying in types and strengths when each one became ineffective as my body acclimatised to it. Today I was taking six different types, twenty tablets over the day, in three doses. I hated being dependent on medication, even more so because it only suppressed the pain, it didn't relieve it.

Suddenly, there was an excitement in me. I was remembering the promise I had been given in 2009 through the pictures of the butterflies that bled on my leg after the muscle biopsy, the promise that 'one day my healing would come.' We talked it through briefly, as Esther was trying to understand where I was coming from. I couldn't explain it, I just knew it. We prayed together and I surrendered to trust God in His plan.

But I am human, and in my excitement, I ran ahead of God, and I stopped taking all of the medication at once. For the next thirty-six hours, I took Holy Communion three times a day, and I believed in God's healing power over my life. But because I had done it my way, my body couldn't cope, and I deteriorated rapidly into a state of collapse. I was beyond coping with the pain in the sudden withdrawal, and I became suicidal in my thoughts. Suddenly, I just didn't want to live.

Esther telephoned to see how I was and immediately dropped everything and came over when she heard my distress. As she came through the door she boldly declared'

"I can agree why it might be forty days, as forty is a very biblical number. There has to be significance why you have to take Communion three times a day, but I did NOT agree with you stopping all of your medication at once!"

As I continued to sob in my distress I told her that I agreed with her. We prayed together, I said sorry to God for running ahead of Him, and I surrendered back into His plan by going back on the medication. I still took Communion three times a day as directed, and I waited for God.

I knew that I had messed up by stopping the medication so suddenly, but what it did prove, however, as if I needed any proof, was that I was chronically sick in head to foot chronic pain, and my body was totally dependent on the medication to enable me to cope!

So as I went to take my first dose of medication on day four, I was surprised to have a sudden hesitation as I held the tablets in my hand. From this point on, God would take me on a journey of obedience and faith in Him that would change my life forever. As I looked at each tablet and prayed, I had a peace to take them all, except one. So I discarded that one tablet and I took the rest. I continued taking Holy Communion and, as I did so, the intimacy and the meaning of it came alive in a whole new way.

Communion is not a ritual, a religious formula or a procedure; it is an invitation from Jesus, a directive to bring our focus into, and to remember, the true meaning of the power of the Cross. As I held the bread in my hand I became aware of the love of Jesus that had been expressed when He chose to go through crucifixion on the Cross. A love so powerful that He was prepared to be whipped mercilessly until His body was ripped to shreds and his bones exposed. A love that caused Him to be stripped, beaten, bruised, spat on, ridiculed, rejected and broken, so that we could be made whole. As I absorbed His love in this remembrance, my faith was enhanced to receive everything that Jesus had died for. He took all our sicknesses and diseases so that we can have health and wholeness in every way, just like Jesus. He did this for me. He did this for you! Embraced in this love, through tears, I believed and I received.

As I drank the wine I remembered how the blood of Jesus, who is perfect, who never did anything wrong, who is the Son of God, was shed for us all. It brought us all forgiveness for every mistake we have ever made, it made us forever 'morally right' again before God, blessed, devoted and blameless. It allows us to speak to God himself, our Father, through Jesus, and His ears are alert to our softest cry. God wants to have a relationship with us, so much so, that He sacrificed His Son, that we might live in freedom and claim eternal life through belief in Jesus.

Jesus always knew that He would suffer and die on the Cross. He boldly went to the Cross, courageously and without any doubt, because He saw what it would mean for you, and for me, today, in this lifetime. He died to set us free from the frailty of our humanity and to give us another chance. He did it for the joy that was to come, beyond the Cross, which allows us to live in freedom today.

As I focused into Communion three times a day, this love washed over me in every dimension of new truth and understanding. I knew I didn't deserve it, but He did it because He is grace, to deliver me from troubles, hardship, distress, and sickness and disease of every kind.

I saw Jesus take my sickness and every frailty from me at the Cross, and give everything that He is in exchange, including a perfect body. And I wept.

For God so loved the world that he gave his one and only Son, that whoever believes in him shall not perish but have eternal life.

John 3:16

19

Obedience

Over the next few days I continued taking all the tablets except the one that I had been shown to discard. All of my tablets had warnings on them similar to this:

> 'Do not stop taking this medication without medical supervision, and only under instruction from a Doctor. It should not be stopped suddenly. It can only be removed on a slow withdrawal by gradually reducing the dose. To do so could cause serious complications.'

But I knew I was in God's hands. He was my divine physician and healer. Taking Holy Communion on my own with Jesus three times a day became exciting, but overwhelming in intimacy as I focused on Him. Incredibly, I had no negative effect from suddenly stopping the tablet, and I began to sense a change in my body.

Within days, I was shown to stop taking another one of the tablets. Over the rest of the forty days, I was shown which tablet to stop, and in which order, sometimes reducing to a half dose first and then stopping it completely. After each tablet was stopped for the last time, He changed nothing for three days and I became aware of more changes in my body.

These are some of the highlight moments from that forty day journey:

Day 6

Today, I was more alert and feeling brighter in myself.

Day 7

Today, I was so alert and began to feel more comfortable all over my body.

Day 9

Today, for the first time in years, I was able to stand up from my wheelchair and I had no pain in my legs! I took my first steps away from the chair and I could slowly walk forward. This was amazing because in the latter days of walking before use of a wheelchair I walked like a crab, sideways, dragging my left leg along the floor as I couldn't lift my foot up off the ground.

Day 10

Today, I had a busy day and usually I would suffer more pain and fatigue because of the exertion, but today I had no negative reaction.

Day 11

Today, I had so much energy I didn't know what to do with it. Suddenly, I was feeling trapped in my home. I had not felt this way about my isolation, ever, in all the twelve years of being sick.

At 2300 hrs, while in bed, I realised that I needed to go to the bathroom. I would never normally get out of bed to do this, especially on my own, but there was no one to help me. So I got out of bed and 'being sensible' I used the electric wheelchair to get to the bathroom. As I got off the chair to walk into the bathroom I was prompted by God through the Holy Spirit to "do something that I have not been able to do before." Don't ask me why, but I bent over and touched my toes. This was risky due to the poor balance that I had had for years, which caused me to walk like a drunk. But tonight, I could touch my toes and stand upright again without falling over. I was so shocked that I did it again. I cannot recall the last time I was able to do that, even before I was sick! I am stunned, excited, amazed and totally blown away by the power of God.

Day 12

Today, I was out all day at a Church event. I wasn't strong enough to walk outside my home yet so I used the electric wheelchair. Again I had no pain, no fatigue and no negative kickback from the exertion.

Day 13

Today, I overslept, because the carer thought I would be so exhausted from my busy day yesterday, that she would let me have a sleep in to recover, and then shower me on her next visit of the day. But it was Sunday and I wanted to go to Church, so I was disappointed (though I did appreciate her consideration). But then I was stirred to attempt to sort myself out. I was able to shower, dress and eat breakfast in just forty five minutes! It was normally a two hour routine with one hour of help from my carer. I enjoyed Church and, on returning home, I had so much energy that I pottered around doing small jobs in my flat.

Day 14

Today, my daughter came home and her boyfriend came to visit. Although it was still early days, I had become so used to getting up from my chair and walking slowly around my flat that I just didn't think anything of it. They were sitting on the couch having a snack, I went walkabout and came back into the room with a dry floor mop to dust the wooden floor in preparation for the group coming over that night. I would have normally sat down on my electric wheelchair and reversed across the room, pulling the mop across the floor to clean it, but today, I was on my feet swinging the pole to the left and right in a sweeping motion as I walked backwards across the room. As I approached the couch where they were sitting, they both lifted their legs up straight out in front of them for me to dust underneath their feet. Only as I walked out of the room did it occur to me that they had not even noticed that I was walking. I was bursting to point out the obvious, but something cautioned me not to.

That evening the Monday Bible Study Group came to meet as usual in my home. A cable became disconnected on the television at the other side of the room when I was showing a DVD. I would have normally asked someone to help to sort it out for me, but without thinking, I walked across the room to do it myself and then returned to my seat. There were ten other people in the room that night, but no one noticed what I had just done, except Esther, who knew what God was doing. It was then that I realised: GOD

WAS KEEPING ME HIDDEN FROM VIEW UNTIL
HE HAD COMPLETED WHAT HE WAS DOING!

Day 15

Today, I had so much energy and freedom to walk that I
cleaned the flat for the first time on my own, even being
active enough to perspire, and I hadn't moved quickly enough
to do that in years!

Day 17

Today, I was standing up listening to a worship song and
praising Jesus for everything that He is, and all He had come
to mean to me in my life, not least for the release taking
place in my body day by day. In a moment of surrender, I
found myself rotating round the room with my arms out,
dancing in His presence, and I cried, overcome with the awe
of who He is and because I could move so freely. His love,
His grace, His mercy, the power of the Cross that He died
on to set us free, and there were no words that I could speak
to express the gratitude that I felt in my heart towards Him
for everything. Oh, the intimacy of His love and grace, there
is just no one like Him! I was so aware of His presence in
the room, and it was as though He danced with me, and as
I twirled, I had perfect balance.

That evening, I was going to a Church event with Esther.
I texted her to ask if she would come ten minutes earlier to
pick me up. As she arrived I put on the worship song I had
danced to that morning and suggested we had a worship
time together. So far into the song, I began to dance. I have
never heard Esther scream in excitement before, but in that
moment it was a piercing, shrill sound of rejoicing and more
tears as she celebrated my freedom with me.

Day 19

Today, my morning carer, Lydia, noticed that there was something different about me as I moved so freely from my bed to go to the bathroom, and again as I moved to stand up away from my wheelchair. I used the chair first thing in the morning to ease my body into the day, but then walked whenever able after that. She was so excited and our conversations in Jesus went to a different level. My other carer remained blind to the situation until after the forty days were completed.

Day 20

Today, Veronica arrived to help me to go to Church this morning. I still didn't have strength to walk outside yet. As she waited for me to finish getting ready she observed me walking out of my bedroom into the hallway carrying my coat, and suddenly, the blinkers were off and she realised what was happening. She was so overwhelmed, overjoyed and excited, she sobbed uncontrollably for a while before being able to speak. I shared some of my journey with her and she almost couldn't believe what she was seeing, or what I was saying, but it was obvious that something had changed. She agreed not to tell anyone as we went down to Church, as I still knew I was being kept hidden for the moment, but the knowing look between us as we smiled together in worship was almost contagious.

Today was Communion Sunday and I looked forward to that moment with God. But today our Minister, Jeff, decided to do it in a way he had never done it before. Usually, we stayed in our seats and it was brought to us, but he was asking that we go to the front, one by one, to take it for ourselves. He also offered that if we would like prayer we should take time to pray for each other in this moment. When people move around in the confined aisles of a Church, it is dangerous to manoeuvre amongst them in an electric wheelchair, so I stayed where I was and I asked Veronica if she would bring the Communion to me, and she agreed to do so.

But God had other ideas. I saw Jeff gesture to a lady across the room to indicate if she would join him in bringing Communion to me. I knew they would pray for me, and probably for my healing, but they had no idea what God was already doing. What was I to do? I knew that I had to be honest, but I also knew that it had to be kept discreet. As they gave me the two elements of Communion, I was then asked what I would like prayer for; though they said they probably knew.

I then asked if I could share something with them in strictest confidence, and they agreed. As I shared a little of what I had been doing Jeff suddenly reacted, almost in disbelief, "You are doing what?!" I reassured him I was okay. In fact, I felt so well that if I knew I had the freedom to do so, I would willingly get off the wheelchair to show him, but I knew it wasn't God's timing yet. But we definitely needed to talk! They agreed not to say anything, prayed a simple prayer of blessing and left me to continue with the service.

Jeff visited me at home four days later and got the shock of his life when I answered the door to him myself, standing up and walking normally. It was a joy to share the journey so far, and he was so excited but in awe of God too. He made a note of the date that my 40 days would be completed, and we both knew I would not be able to keep the secret anymore after that day.

Day 21

Over the years, everyone came to know that they should never touch my body because I was in so much pain. British people are notorious for embracing in a hug and while doing so, patting you between the shoulder blades as though they are helping a baby to get their wind up. So many times I had to refrain from yelping in pain as people would do this to me, either not recognising, or just forgetting my physical distress.

Today, my three-year-old granddaughter decided to climb on my chair and stand behind me, something she had never done before. Suddenly, she threw her arms around my neck from behind and pressed her body hard into my back, and I was amazed that it didn't hurt! She then proceeded to climb up to sit on my shoulders and that didn't hurt either, and I was amazed. She then insisted that I stand up and show her what we look like in the mirror. I hesitated, but then I thought, why not? I was able to stand up with her on my shoulders, walk to the mirror, and I took a 'selfie' of our reflection to prove it! That evening, it was Bible study group time again. As I sang in worship I could hear my own audible voice for the first time in fifteen months. Esther was able to hear it too from across the room, but everyone else was oblivious! Then, as I began to speak out to teach in the Bible study, I again had no voice and I had to use the microphone again to amplify my whisper. It wasn't time for other people to know anything yet.

Every day was a physical strengthening and I knew that my whole demeanour had changed from being 'woolly headed' because of the medication side effects to being mentally alert and able to think straight for the first time in years. I wasn't stiff in my joints or muscles and I didn't have to take a long time to get my body moving in the morning after a night in bed. I didn't have pain anywhere in my body despite the removal of the painkillers. I could eat more easily as my swallowing reflex came back. The tremor disappeared. I didn't have any negative 'kick back' after exertion.

For years, I had had to 'pace' myself, and choose what I was prepared to suffer for. If I did something out of normal routine one day, I knew I had to give myself three or four days to recover before I could consider doing something else. I was so excited, but I was in awe of all that was happening.

I went from strength to strength over these few days. Two more friends, Jessica and Pamela, came to visit individually and noticed that there was something different about me, not least, the energy that was now reflected in my eyes that had looked so 'spaced out' and lifeless for so long. They were so excited and could barely keep what I showed them to themselves.

I was intrigued how some people would begin to see for themselves and yet so many were kept blind until the end. But then I began to understand something more of human nature. When we look, what do we see? If we are only looking at ourselves and our own situations, we become so distracted and inner focused that we can become closed down to anything else going on around us. How blind are we? How many times do we 'look' but do not see the obvious that is happening? How much do we look at things and just accept how they are, and never believe for things to change, that when change happens we are numb to the process? How much do we rob ourselves and others by our limited vision of understanding? However...

Day 29

Today, it was Tuesday, so Esther and I were having a time of worship and prayer together. There came a point when all I wanted to do was to kneel in honour of who God is, but I had not been able to kneel for many years. I reached a point when I could no longer stand, not because my legs were weak, but because of the presence of God. In a moment

I was kneeling on the floor, totally surrendered, overwhelmed and in awe, and I leaned forward over my chair and put my head on my arms and absolutely broke, sobbing uncontrollably with so many different emotions. So thankful for the breakthrough, so grateful to be able to move in this way again, so loved, so free, so humbled that I was experiencing Jesus in this powerful way and yet beginning to question, why me? As I recovered my composure, I then sat cross-legged on the floor in prayer.

I was totally oblivious to what Esther was doing during this time. The next day I received photographs on my mobile phone that Esther had taken in that moment the day before. She had been so shocked to see me kneeling that she captured the moment on camera. To see me sitting on the floor was sheer elation as she witnessed my continued journey to freedom. Maybe it pays to keep our eyes open in prayer!

Day 33

Tonight my daughter Kaitlin is at home, jet-lagged after one of her business trips. As she lay on the couch to relax, she dropped something on the floor. I stood up to retrieve it for her so that she wouldn't have to move. As I did so, she suddenly asked. "What are you doing differently?"

I asked what she meant? For years I have been in so much pain that I struggled to hold my body upright. I would normally recline backward in my chair so that my whole body, neck, and head were adequately supported. But tonight, I moved easily to pick something up off the floor for her, and she can see me sitting bolt upright, and not supported by the chair at all in my upper body. So what have I been doing differently?

As she has now asked questions, I knew it was the right time to show her what has changed in my body. I stood up from my chair, and I walked across the room in front of her before returning to sit down again. Her eyes followed me, but she was not registering what I was doing. So I walked across the room again and then pirouetted back to my chair, and I stood there waiting for her reaction. For a moment she looked puzzled, and I was about to bend and touch my toes as the final demonstration of my freedom, when she suddenly protested, "Don't you dare attempt to touch your toes when you are not wearing your emergency call button!"

God has a sense of humour. For years I had been using the same emergency call equipment that used to be my job to install for frail and elderly people. It had given peace of mind to everyone that I could call help easily in an emergency when I was on my own. But I had not put it on today, and Kaitlin could see it was on my bookcase close to my chair.

As I bent to touch my toes I laughed out loud. My first thought was, 'Well if I was to fall over, you could press the button!' But I refrained from comment and sat down. Kaitlin then asked again, "What have you been doing differently," but then proceeded to say, "And don't tell me a 'God' story."

I sat quietly for a moment. I believe in Jesus, He is the centre of my life, and though my children were all raised in their early childhood to go to Church, they had all decided in their teenage years that they didn't want to go anymore. They respected my journey with God, and I had to respect their choices. They know we often differ on understanding and opinions of life choices that people make, but it doesn't divide us to cause breakdown of relationship. I love my children beyond measure. I am so proud of them all in the individuality of who they are, and all that they achieve in life. I pray for them. I trust God for them. As I hesitated to respond in this moment, Kaitlin knew my dilemma, and as I then said I couldn't explain without speaking about God, she gave me permission to share, but NOT to "Make it a long one!" I couldn't help but smile. At least she was being honest, and that same heart responded in no uncertain terms as I shared a brief summary of the last thirty-three days.

Knowing I had stopped the medication, she asked if my doctor knew what I was doing. As I answered that he didn't know at the moment, but I had an appointment booked to see him in three weeks time, she suddenly became angry. Didn't I know that what I was doing was so dangerous!? Many celebrities have died coming off drugs of many kinds without medical supervision and she was too young to lose her mum!

Her next concern was, "You do know that if you are healed all your welfare benefits will stop and you will have nothing to live on."

And then a final consideration on that same point: "Mum, you haven't worked properly for twelve years and you are coming up for your sixtieth birthday next year. You are totally unemployable!"

My heart went out to my daughter in all her mixed emotions. I understood her fear of losing her mum, and how could I expect her to understand that I was in safe hands with Jesus, when at the moment she wasn't on that same journey? Yes, I understood that my financial position would change and I wouldn't be able to afford things like the rent and bills on my home, but this was no surprise to Jesus, and He would have a plan for that too. As for being so unemployable because of my lack of recent experience and age? I had known for many years that one day I would work full time for Jesus. I didn't know how it was ever going to happen, but perhaps I was becoming a little more understanding towards it now.

These last twelve years were not about me being stripped and destroyed. They were a learning journey in Jesus that would equip and enable me to do whatever God had planned for me in my future. My confidence was in Him. He would continue to lead me step by step. He would not abandon me now.

In all these fears that came into her conversation with me, Kaitlin struggled to rejoice with me in my freedom. But at least now she knew the truth. I did ask that at this point would she please keep it to herself, trust that I was absolutely okay, and believe that my recovery would be completed as soon as the forty days came to an end. Seven days to go. Then, we could tell her brothers.

Three days later Kaitlin came home from work and embraced me in tears. Apologising for her angry outburst when I had shown her that I was becoming well again, she said she couldn't understand it, but she couldn't deny it either; she could see so much improvement and I looked so well. She was excited and elated at the prospect of "having her mum back again." I reassured her everything was going to be okay. I wasn't upset by her reaction and I couldn't expect her to understand it the way I did through faith, but the only explanation is the healing power of God!

Day 38

Today was my first day without any medication to take. I took my last tablet for the last time yesterday. I had no ill effect from being removed from the tablets. As I woke up in the morning and said my usual, "Good morning" to God, my voice came out in its normal strength and tone; it was so loud I was shocked, and for a moment I thought someone else was in the room! And yes, I was in awe, overwhelmed at this final moment of release, and there was jubilant celebration in more tears in thankfulness to God. He had completed what He had started.

Day 40

I AM PAIN FREE, I HAVE NO FATIGUE, I CAN WALK, I CAN DANCE, I CAN SIT ON THE FLOOR, I CAN KNEEL, I CAN TOUCH MY TOES, I HAVE A VOICE, I CAN SPEAK, I CAN SING, I CAN EAT NORMALLY, I CAN PICK UP AND HOLD MY GRANDCHILDREN IN MY ARMS.
I AM HEALED! THANK YOU JESUS!

> By faith in the name of Jesus, this man whom you see and know was made strong. It is Jesus' name and the faith that comes through him that has completely healed him, as you can all see.
>
> **Acts 3:16**

> Yet he did not waver through unbelief regarding the promise of God, but was strengthened in his faith and gave glory to God, [21] being fully persuaded that God had power to do what He had promised.
>
> **Romans 4:20-21**

This whole episode of my life, not least the last forty days, has been a journey of faith. Faith that believed in the name of Jesus, faith that believed in the power of the Cross, faith that believed that God was directing my steps, faith to obey what I knew that God was asking me to do, even though it didn't make sense. Faith to trust day by day, faith to admit that I had run ahead in the beginning, but as I re-tracked back into His plan...faith to know that God is a God of second chances (and more): Faith to believe God's promises, faith to surrender to receive, faith to see and know Jesus in a deeper way, faith to believe for my healing and my future. Faith in nothing else - except the healing power of Jesus!

After twelve years of being chronically sick, including seven years being wheelchair dependent, and totally losing my voice for fifteen months – I HAVE BEEN SET FREE!

WARNING

For anyone who has ill health and may be taking presecribed medications:

This is a very personal account of my journey as I was led by the Holy Spirit power of God. By sharing this detail, I am not in any way suggesting, prompting, advising or recommending, that anyone else should copy or imitate what I was led to do. To do so would be very dangerous and could have life threatening consequences.

If you have a personal relationship with God, be encouraged, believe for His healing grace in your life, and let Him do it His way.

THE ONLY WAY OUT IS THROUGH....

The only way to get on the other side of a problem and eliminate its power over you is to face it and allow the Holy Spirit to instruct you in your heart and in the Word on how to walk through it.

But the Comforter, which is the Holy Ghost, whom the Father will send in my name, he shall teach you all things, and bring all things to your remembrance, whatsoever I have said unto you.

John 14:26 King James Version

Joyce Meyer (Daily Calendar)

20

Breakthrough Freedom

I was free, totally healed and about to go to the next level in many ways, and other people were about to be shocked, challenged and changed in their understanding of many things. Especially their faith in God.

The same evening that the forty days were completed, I was to babysit for my son Charles and his wife Elaine. Despite all of my difficulties, I was so blessed, that they had allowed me to help them in this way over the years, knowing that if there had been any difficulties I would call on them to come home immediately to assist. I praise God that there were never any problems, I never had to call them, and I built up a precious relationship with my beautiful grandchildren.

They were born when I was mostly wheelchair dependent and they had never known me to be any other way. They knew I stayed in my chair, and that they had to come to me to play with their toys. They could sit on my knee and I did one to one creative things with them. They always had my undivided attention and they loved it. I was never busy doing other things.

It was a novelty to ride on my knee on the electric wheelchair from room to room if I had to go to the kitchen, and my riser recliner chair made a great slide if I raised it to the stand-up position with them sitting on it! Visits to me were different; they loved my disability gadgets. My 'grabber stick', an aid to help me to pick up anything I had dropped on the floor, was a useful fishing rod to pick up paper clip 'fishes' using the magnet that was located on the end.

But there was also an incredible sensitivity, particularly from my grandson Jeremy. From the moment he learned to walk, if he saw me attempt to stand up in the room (to manoeuvre from wheelchair to another chair) he would immediately drop whatever he was playing with and run over, reach out to hold my hand, and say "Jeremy help." I would well up in tears every single time at his gentle, compassionate heart and willingness to help me from such a young age.

In my grandchildren's younger years as babies and toddlers, my friends would often assist me to look after them during the day as I couldn't run around after them. But once they were in bed, they slept through the night and I was able to cope on my own. Those friends gave me precious memories that I treasure forever, an easy way to enjoy my grandchildren growing up. But I also had incredible heartache as I watched someone else sitting on the floor and playing with my grandchild in a way that I never could.

But tonight, Jeremy aged five years and Laura aged three, were coming for a sleep over. As we texted arrangements to each other, I asked their parents to come over one hour earlier, as I had something to tell them. As they arrived the children were excited as they came through the door. Jeremy was trying to take his coat and shoes off at the same time. As I said, "Hello Jeremy" he heard my voice and froze in mid movement, arms raised but trapped in his coat sleeves, and one foot raised to shake off his shoe, almost like the 'crane' stance performed in the film 'Karate Kid'. He just looked at me in disbelief, then his mum Elaine shouted: "Did I just hear your voice?"

I asked them to come and sit down and I began to share what had happened. The children sat quietly on the couch, listening intently to every word that I said, and watching my every movement. Their mum nearly fell off her chair and squealed in shock and delight as I got up and walked across the room, and then I bent over to touch my toes. I explained about sitting on the floor, my new energy and how my voice returned. Charles sat quietly, and I could see his emotions beginning to stir, but he said nothing.

Since his formative years, he had always carried his emotions deep, using humour to hide his feelings. So I was waiting for the wisecracks to be made, but he said nothing as he pondered quietly, and I am moved by his response.

As their parents left them with me for their 'sleepover with Nanna,' the children were excited as they said "goodnight" and waved their parents goodbye. But Jeremy didn't move from the couch. As soon as the front door was closed behind his parents, he asked, "Nanna, can you really sit on the floor to play with me now?"

"Yes Jeremy, I can."

He asked, "Can you show me?"

I sat cross-legged on the floor as his eyes went wide in amazement. But he was so touched by his emotions that he couldn't move. Laura immediately ran towards me and sat on my lap in sheer delight. Realising his awe, I asked Jeremy to come and sit on the floor with us and suggested that we could take a 'selfie' to send to his parents, to show them I can sit on the floor. He approached in excited trepidation and sat down beside me. I embraced him and took a photograph of the three of us together.

He then rotated onto his knees to look me in the eye, and with obvious concern asked, "Nanna, are you able to get back up again? Do you want me to help you?"

I was choked at the heart of compassion and concern that he continued to express so openly. I thanked him for being willing to help, reassured him that I could get up by myself, and proceeded to show him. That evening was a joy to behold of free movement around them, their acceptance that I had been healed by Jesus, and Jeremy seeing the possibilities ahead of us in the different things we would now be able to do. Within a few short weeks, I would take them to the park on my own for the first time and push them on the swings!

Their dad came to pick them up the following day, and having had a night to ponder what he had seen and heard, he was emotional as he embraced me, so thrilled to have his mum back. He didn't understand it, but could not deny the radicle turnaround in my life!

Over time to come, I would understand more of what it really meant to him that I was now free. I was able to join in on family events more easily because we didn't have to consider a wheelchair for access in restaurants and other public places. We would all be sitting around chatting and having a meal together when out of the corner of my eye, I would catch him staring at me with a beaming grin from across the room. I would look at him quizzically, and he would just smile and shake his head as though in disbelief. He was so excited that I could join in and do 'normal' things again with the family, without consideration of a wheelchair. And so was I!

There was one thing that both Kaitlin and Charles both agreed on: I could not tell their brother Lawrence over the telephone! He would never comprehend or believe it unless he could see it for himself. I could see their point of view, and as much as I didn't like to keep him in the dark when his siblings knew the truth, I knew they were right, and it was necessary that I make arrangements for that overseas trip to happen as soon as I was able, and so it was booked for twelve days later.

The next day was a Sunday and I attended Church. It was still too far for me to walk there, so I had to use the electric wheelchair and was escorted by Esther. As was a frequent event, today our church was set out in a 'Café style,' small tables surrounded by circles of chairs positioned around the room. It was a family service and setting up in this way promoted a more relaxed environment for families to unite together around drinks and nibbles, and craft activities were available for the children to do in-keeping with the theme of the morning's message that Jeff would bring.

Due to the very nature of the way that the seating was set up, I was to sit at a table at the back of the room as there was no space for my wheelchair to manoeuvre anywhere else. We had a great time together as we focused on the simplicity of the message and family time. Once the main activities were over, Jeff announced, "Before we go, Grace would like to share something with us."

As I slowly moved my body to stand up from my wheelchair, I could hear the shuffle of people looking around to see what was happening. I let my outdoor jacket fall off from my arms onto the wheelchair so that I was able to move more freely, and then I began to walk very slowly through the middle of the chairs towards Jeff at the front of the room. There was an audible gasp from some people as they began to comprehend what was happening. Others reached out their hands or arms towards me as I approached them - a safety measure in case I needed to steady myself as I walked by. I stayed focused on Jeff and walked slowly to the front, and as I reached the lectern, I turned around to see the room of people from a standing position for the first time, and I was overwhelmed.

I quickly pulled myself together and then I began to speak. The shock, as they could hear my audible voice for the first time in over fifteen months, was evident on their faces as I briefly began to tell them about the journey that

God had taken me through for the last forty days. Many were in tears - both men and women - whilst others had the biggest smiles I have ever seen, and they all listened intently as I shared my news. But then, there were others who were poker-faced, as though not comprehending or understanding what had just happened. Such a mixed emotion running throughout the room and yet such excitement. Those who had already seen evidence of my progressive healing couldn't help but be excited at the public release of my news and were vocal in their responses, yet others were emotionless as they watched me prove that I could touch my toes and freely manoeuvre my body. As I announced, "I am totally pain-free, I no longer have chronic fatigue, I no longer take any medication, I can speak again, and declared, I AM HEALED IN JESUS' NAME," people stood up clapping and cheering and again I was in tears.

Without my knowing, Jeff had organised for a YouTube video to be played as a final song of worship to end the meeting. It was the very song through which I had been released to dance and kneel in worship during my progressive healing. As I sang, I danced, and others joined me as they surrounded me at the front of the Church, and we worshipped our God, who is so faithful.

The song: This Is Our God, *(by Hillsong)*

The lyrics begin:

> *Your grace is enough*
> *More than I need*
> *At Your word I will believe*
> *I wait for You*
> *Draw near again*
> *Let Your spirit make me new*

Conversations with some people were 'electric' afterward as people were in awe of God and His healing grace. I stood around answering questions as people felt able to freely speak out, and many were tearful. They had been praying that I would be healed for many years, and now to see their prayers answered was amazing, but more so, to marvel at how God had chosen to do it; He had just defied all logic and understanding, but it had made them realise just how much we limit God with our human thinking and restriction on how we pray.

The breakthrough had come and the witness to other people was about to unfold in so many ways. I had crossed paths with so many people in the twelve-year journey, and news would travel fast in my immediate neighbourhood. My hair is now quite striking in colour as a result of doing a fund raising event for charity two years earlier. Unable to run a marathon, I had allowed Kaitlin to use her professional skills to style my hair into a 'mohican' and colour it in the seven colours of the rainbow! It was well worth it for the monies raised, but it left me with a dilemma on how to have something more 'normal' afterward. We eventually settled on a raspberry purple colour on the top, with my natural grey at the sides – I am not in denial of my age or my grey hair!

I became known as the 'lady with the purple hair in the wheelchair.' Once I was able to begin walking around the local streets to build up muscle capacity and stamina, people used to recognise me because of my hair and they were curious as to why I could now walk. As I explained, many would hug me, weep and be overjoyed at what they were able to witness, and some turned their lives back to Jesus!

But my immediate concern was to show my family, especially my mum. It was now time to go back home to my birth family to show them what God has done.

Come and hear, all you who fear God; let me tell you what he has done for me.

Psalm 66:16

Jesus did not let him, but said, "Go home to your own people and tell them how much the Lord has done for you, and how he has had mercy on you."

Mark 5:19

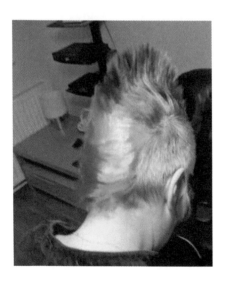

21

Shall We Dance?

It has always amazed me just how God orders our steps, and His timing is always perfect. My family lives two hundred and thirty miles away in the North East of England. Back in August, Esther had kindly offered that if I would like to visit my mum and family before Christmas, she was more than willing to take me, but preferably during November, as December is always such a busy month. Esther had supported me in this way many times over the years and had become very much accepted as part of the family in so many ways. So, in order to take advantage of early booking accommodation rates, we had duly booked to go on 20th November.

I was born one of eight children, and my mum was still alive aged 91 years, but she was frail with dementia. In the loss of my voice, it had been heartbreaking, as I could no longer speak to my mum on the telephone. We had talked together so much over the years and, as I had gone through the difficulties, Mum would repeatedly ask, "Is there nothing that they can do for you?" in reference to the hospital services. I used to reassure her that they were doing their best, but we need to pray and believe for a miracle. She would chuckle and say, "Yes, I believe for a miracle. I say my prayers for my children every night."

Little did we know when booking that weekend trip so far in advance, that the weekend before, we would see the completion of my healing. So this trip was going to allow my family to see what God had done. I didn't know how they were going to respond. Only one of my sisters attends a church, and the rest of my siblings would only go for weddings, christenings, and funerals, or 'hatch', 'match' and 'dispatch', as they were known.

For the first time in twelve years, I was able to walk into my brother's home where my mum lived. Believing I was still wheelchair dependent, one of my brothers came out to the car to help me as we pulled up to the driveway. The look of amazement on his face as he saw me walk away from the car was a delight to see. He didn't know what to say, and as I grinned at him, neither did I. We went into the house together and he didn't say a word. As I walked into the lounge I was emotional to see my mum. She looked so frail and, as dementia is so unpredictable and cruel, I wasn't sure if she would recognise me or remember who I was. But the sudden smile on her face said more than any words can ever express of her joy to see me again, and then she said my name. I walked across the room, approached her in tears, and as I bent down to embrace her, she asked, "What are you doing here?"

As my tears subsided, I was eventually able to speak softly into her ear and say, "You know that miracle we have both been praying for? Well, I have come to show you the answer to our prayers." Her eyes came alive as she said, "Really?" I stepped away from her and said, "Look, Mum, I can walk. And can you hear that? The sound of my voice has come back!" As the truth impacted, I saw tears begin to roll down her cheeks, and through her smile, she said, "He has answered our prayers. He has done a miracle." In that one lucid moment, we had a connection, and my mum knew that I was healed. Sadly, as anyone who deals with dementia might know, that lucid moment passed quite quickly, and Mum went back into her own world. But I praise God that she understood in that moment and she was overjoyed and thankful.

I saw all seven of my brothers and sisters over that weekend and many of my nieces and nephews. Everyone was emotional but ecstatic at what they could see and hear. They had worried for so long about my poor health and had questioned after every visit whether this might be the last time that they might see me because I was deteriorating so fast. So many questions were asked as I explained what had happened. It was difficult for them to take on board just 'how' it had happened. I could only bare witness in truth; it was up to them what they would choose to do with it. They have a free will choice on what to believe. They couldn't explain it, but they couldn't deny it either! Everyone was elated to see me walking in such freedom. It was early days, but I would very quickly go from strength to strength.

A group of us went out for a meal together, where we were joined by my eldest brother Mark. As he saw us pull up in the car park at the restaurant on a bitterly cold winter evening, he came out to help me so that I wouldn't slip on the frosty ground. I stood up out of the car and took the arm that he offered, and when I reassured him that I didn't need the wheelchair, we began to walk slowly to the entrance. There came a point where we had to walk through a narrow gap between two parked cars, I unlinked my arm from him and I was the first to walk through the gap. I then proceeded to walk straight into the building without looking back. It took a moment to realise that he had not followed me. He caught up a few moments later at the table where I was now seated, and protested, "What on earth was that? What just happened? I came out into the freezing cold to help you from the car, and then you were able to walk away from me, leaving me standing!" We all laughed and I began to explain everything to him. My brother is a confident, talkative and world travelled man, but tonight, he was stuck for words. He spent the rest of the evening looking at me in disbelief, repeatedly saying that he could not believe what he has seen, but he couldn't deny it either!

We stayed in the hotel one more night to prepare for the long drive home the following day. Early next morning I received a phone call to say that my Mum had been admitted to the hospital overnight with suspected heart problems. There was a history of previous heart attack so I didn't know what to expect. Although it was outside of normal visiting hours, the hospital kindly agreed to let Esther and I visit her before we left town. It was a long walk through the hospital to where they said Mum was, so we used the push wheelchair to speed things up. On the way, we passed the Chapel and the door was open. I asked if we could go in for a moment and Esther obliged.

On the main wall was a Cross, either side of the Cross were two banners, each with a dove at the top, and I knew God was getting my attention. I wear a ring that was given to me by my parents in 2005. It has a Cross on it with a dove either side, and it has the Lord's Prayer imprinted on the inside of the ring. God knew the cry of my heart over the years. Did my Mum really believe in Jesus? When she dies, will she be in eternity in Heaven? When she departs this lifetime, will I see her again? There was a banner across the front of a table at the altar, with a picture of a dove and the words 'Be Still'. We spent a couple of moments in prayer and left the room with incredible peace.

In her dementia confusion, Mum was agitated, disorientated and distressed, because she wasn't in the familiarity of her own home. I reassured her as I watched the nurses carry out their tests. I was very mindful that we didn't know how much longer Mum would live. I knew that she had repeatedly said over the years that she prayed for her children, but I had never known her to attend church. I was surprised as suddenly, without prompting, she opened up a conversation with us both about her childhood. How she had gone to Sunday school because her mum had insisted, how her mum had taught her how to pray, and how those prayers had been for her children all these years.

Esther then asked her, "Do you know Psalm 23 in the Bible?"

Mum answered, "Yes, I know Psalm 23" and then proceeded to repeat it boldly and confidently from memory, absolutely word perfect! As I watched and listened, I was overwhelmed as I choked back my tears.

The nurses came to take her blood pressure, so I backed away from the bed to the middle of the ward to give them space, and I watched Mum in her dementia playing up like a naughty little girl, saying she didn't want them to touch her, and sticking her tongue out behind their back. It was funny, but it wasn't; it was sad, dementia is just so cruel. As I fought my tears I began to pray in the middle of the ward. *Lord, I have heard her quote words from the Bible, but I need to know that my Mum truly believes, that her heart belongs to you.*

Suddenly, my mum raised her left arm in the air and pointed to the ceiling, looking me in the eye as she protested loudly:

"I BELIEVE IN JESUS. HE DIED ON THE CROSS THAT I MIGHT LIVE. I WENT TO CHURCH AND SUNDAY SCHOOL WITH MY MUM WHEN I WAS A CHILD. MY MUM TAUGHT ME HOW TO PRAY AND I COVER MY CHILDREN IN PRAYER EVERY NIGHT."

I am overwhelmed at her public confession and God's answer to my prayer. I go back to the bed, embrace my mum, and there is a peace over her as we spend a little while longer together. Esther very kindly took photographs of us together. I repeatedly tell her that I love her, and she keeps saying that she loves me, she loves all of her children and is so proud of every one of us.

As it came time for us to leave, Esther asked Mum if it was okay to say a prayer before we leave. Mum says, "Yes" and without prompting, confidently leads us all in the Lord's Prayer together. The intimacy is profound. I embrace her, telling her again that I love her, and we leave.

That was the last conversation I would ever have with my mum, the last time I ever saw my mum alive. Thirty five days later she passed away in her own home, into the arms of Jesus and eternal rest. God is faithful.

Two days after returning home, I attended the pre-booked appointment with my doctor. I had last seen him when I was still in my physical frailty, approximately two weeks before my healing journey began. He had been concerned about my blood pressure, but he had chosen to monitor it rather than prescribe medication because of all the other tablets I was taking.

Today, as he came to his surgery door and called out my name, I stood up and walked confidently towards him. His eyes went wide open with surprise, and as I walked past him into the room I said in my normal voice, "Good morning." His jaw dropped open and he froze on the spot. Eventually, in shock, he asked me to take a seat. I tried to lighten the moment a little by asking "Could I use one of these chairs for a change?" As I gestured towards the normal chairs at the side of his desk. I had never sat in a patient's chair before as I was always in my wheelchair!

He sat down and asked, "What on earth has happened to you since I last saw you?"

I replied, "Do you remember when we first met five years ago and I said, 'I am not in denial of my medical condition, but one day I will walk into this room, I will not need a wheelchair, I will be pain free, totally healed, and I will dance?'

And "Do you remember your reply?" Well today, I have come to claim my dance!

He smiled as he clearly remembered, but again asked what had happened?

I shared in very simple terms the journey that I had taken, explaining a little of the Christian meaning of Holy Communion. As I explained my physical recovery, step by step through the forty days, I watched this precious man go through every emotion imaginable as he tried to comprehend how this could be. He said that as I was speaking, every hair on his body was standing on end. Eventually, the tears came.

Once he had recovered himself he advised that he would not take my blood pressure because:

'Today, everybody's blood pressure would be up because of the excitement of what I had just shared.'

But also, if my blood pressure was slightly raised he would feel medically obliged to intervene, and he could not touch what was going on in my body right now.

I could see that he knew that my turnaround had nothing to do with medical science. It could not be explained, and he may not understand it, but he was in reverent awe and knew it could not be explained by human logic. He knew he could not interfere with God's plan.

After further discussion and elation in what he was now witnessing, he was so excited. He had never experienced anything like it before and was almost beyond words. But then he stood up and asked, "Shall we dance?" I laughed and said yes, standing up to do so, and we waltzed briefly around the room in celebration.

I had taken Esther on the appointment with me as a chaperone to protect us both in our doctor/patient relationship, as a witness for the glory of God!

Now this is eternal life: that they know you, the only true God, and Jesus Christ, whom you have sent.

John 17:3

Whoever believes in the Son has eternal life, but whoever rejects the Son will not see life, for God's wrath remains on them.

John 3:36

I know that many people reading this book may not yet believe in Jesus. I include these two verses because they are truth in the word of God.

People often ask me how I came to follow Jesus, but more importantly, why do I understand what the Bible is saying. I liken it to anything that we may choose to follow.

If you are interested in football, it is likely that you have a favourite team. As you follow that team you learn new facts about them as a team, as individual players, what games they play, how they play, did they win or lose, where they are placed in the league etc.

Because you are interested, you take time to follow them and find out and understand what you want to know.

Well, it is the same for me in my faith journey. I came to Jesus in 1985 and I knew in that moment that I had a choice, and I chose to say "Yes, I believe He is the Son of God, I believe He died on the Cross for me, that whatever I have done wrong I can be forgiven if I admit it. I believe I am so loved by Him and that God has a plan for my life that is not dependent on me being perfect; it is because He is perfect and He has already prepared the way for me to go forward with Him, through faith in His Son Jesus.

But, unless I accepted Him, and gave Him permission to be in my life, God could not do what He wanted to do in me and for me. By faith in Jesus, I know this life is not the 'be all' and 'end all' of all things. When we die there is Heaven or Hell waiting for us. Heaven is for those who believe in Jesus. Hell is for those who do not.

As I focus on who God is and study the Bible, I learn more every day as the Holy Spirit gives me understanding, and it is just so exciting!

The difference between following a football team and following Jesus is that football has an end - to the game, to individual careers and when they are not doing well, to your interest. But Jesus died on the Cross, came back to life, and did it all because of love and grace, that by believing in Him, we can overcome death too. My relationship with Him will go on forever, even in eternity.

That is why I am so excited that my mum died believing in Jesus! My mum was far from perfect, just the same as me.

But our eternal journey is not dependent on who we are, but on who Jesus is.

Perhaps you have never really considered who God is, or who Jesus is. I encourage you to look into the Bible for yourself. Find someone you know who has a faith in Jesus and start asking questions. Go step by step and be curious about the possibilities. Open yourself up to new under- standing and new opportunities. It is never too late, and I know you will be pleasantly surprised. God loves you. God is faithful. He will not let you down. You really have nothing to lose, but everything to gain!

PART SEVEN

FREEDOM

22

From Strength to Strength

As each day went by I was getting progressively stronger, but I had to pace myself so that I didn't try to run before I could walk. Twelve years of chronic sickness and many years in a wheelchair had obviously weakened my muscles and reduced my stamina, but now, through everyday living, my strength capacity was being slowly built up. The freedom of having no pain in my body was exhilarating, to say the least!

The day finally came for me to visit my son Lawrence and his family in Europe. I travelled by myself but used the 'escorted flight' service that airlines offer to make travel possible for people who are elderly, or physically limited in some way. I cannot fault this amazing service. Esther and her husband kindly drove me to the airport and left me at the appropriate point for assistance. As I still had a limitation on the distance I could walk, it was necessary for me to be pushed in a wheelchair to get from the airport to the plane.

Once on the plane, I was so excited at the prospect of seeing my son again. I had been privileged to spend last Christmas with them when I had used the same escorted flight services to travel. It was such a challenge in my physical decline at that time, that I questioned if that would be the last time that I would be able to see them in their own home. But God had other plans. Here I was today, flying, to show them the miracle turnaround in my body.

I had contacted them through messaging to ask if I could come over and visit, even if it was just for a weekend, before the Christmas holidays. I was missing them and I would love to see the grandchildren. I was trying to be as nonchalant as possible so as not to arouse any suspicion as to what my trip was about. But, despite my best intentions, my request had disturbed my son. His imagination took over and, in conversations with his wife, Lindsey, he was questioning, 'Had I been to the doctor? Was I coming to share bad news about my health? Had I been given a diagnosis? Was the diagnosis genetic? Could it have negative consequences genetically for himself, his siblings, or his children?'

He had so many concerns and worries as to why I wanted to come at such short notice, that Lindsey, out of concern for Lawrence, had telephoned me to check what was going on. As I answered her call she was immediately impacted at hearing the sound of my voice! My loss of voice had meant that all communication with them by telephone had also come to a halt. We had connected occasionally on Skype so that I could listen to them and see the grandchildren, but they couldn't hear me speak.

She explained her concern for Lawrence, and I was torn, but I knew that I had to tell her the truth over the phone. As I shared everything, she broke down and sobbed, so excited, so relieved and with so much love for me, so thankful that I was now so much stronger and well again. I cried too as we discussed the possibility of my visit, and when would it be convenient for them? Lindsey protested, "The timing doesn't matter, just get on a plane and come over as soon as possible. Lawrence needs to see this for himself!" She then agreed that she wouldn't say a word to him; she would reassure him not to worry but would let him see it for himself when he came to pick me up from the airport. I don't like secrets, especially between husband and wife, but this was one time when so much more would be exposed in the moment of truth.

Two plane trips and eleven hours later, I finally arrived at a local airport one hour away from their home. I was met at the door of the plane to be escorted by wheelchair into the arrivals lounge, to wait for my son who had been slightly delayed on his way from work. I was so excited, but nervous in my emotions. How would he cope with what he was about to see?

He arrived ten minutes later and broke into a grin as he saw me sitting in the wheelchair. He kissed me on the cheek and apologised for being late, then he explained that he had to sort the car out to get my case and wheelchair in, as he had forgotten to take his son's buggy out of the boot before going to work that morning, but it wouldn't take long. I stood up from the wheelchair to embrace him in a hug, and in doing so, I spoke to reassure him it is okay, it won't be a problem, as I haven't brought my wheelchair with me.

He commented about being able to hear my voice and he was clearly surprised, but happy. Then he suggested that he would leave me in the airport where it was warm while he sorted the car out for my wheelchair. While still standing up, I repeated again, "I haven't brought my wheelchair as I don't need it now." He looked at the chair I had been sitting in and I reminded him that it belonged to the airport. I calmly said, "I can walk to the car. I just need my case picked up from the luggage collection point behind you. But can I go to the toilet before we leave the airport please?"

I knew he had still not registered what I had said, as he told me to sit down in the wheelchair, and he would push me to the toilet door. I took hold of his arm as I firmly said, "No, let me walk with you to the door." I then proceeded to walk towards the exit of the airport, stopping at the toilets on the way. He was shocked and just didn't know how to respond as I let go of his arm and walked through the door without any help.

As I came out again, I could see that the 'penny had finally dropped' so to speak. He was standing there, feet apart in a confident stance, arms folded across his chest, and grinning at me with the biggest smile that went from ear to ear. I smiled back at my precious son, and yet again the tears began to fall.

As we drove back to his home, we talked intensely as I explained what had happened, and he asked lots of questions to understand everything for himself. He was so excited as we laughed and faced the truth together. Then suddenly, about halfway home, he became emotional. Initially, I suggested that he should pull over to the side of the road so that we could talk. But he continued to drive and, as he did so, he began to talk out his emotions.

He explained how hard it had been to live abroad when I had been so ill. How torn he had sometimes felt as he had watched me deteriorate over the years, and questioned where it was all going to end. His fears over his siblings and his family, if what I had been suffering was a genetic concern for them all, his guilt at not being there for me in the circumstances, not able to practically help in any way. His anger that I didn't deserve to go through what I had suffered after all I did to help so many people, especially my children. His distress that his children couldn't have the relationship with me like they do with his in-laws because of the physical restrictions, even in my not being able to hold them tightly in my arms. So much truth was expressed, and as we cried together, I loved my son for the honesty that he was able to put into words.

It is all about perspective. Everything we go through doesn't just affect us, it touches the lives of everybody connected to us, and it hurts for them to watch what is beyond their control. Some people can express how they feel, others bury it. Now, in this time of honesty and truth, there was a freedom for Lawrence to let go of his pain, to enjoy this moment, to let his fears go, and to begin to believe for the best that was yet to come. Indeed, so much more was exposed because of the secret being kept from him until now. In this moment of truth, as he saw for himself, he was able to confront his emotions, before everyone else would see for themselves too.

Honesty gives freedom to us all. Anything buried alive, our emotions, our resentment, our regret, our bitterness, our anger, our fears, will inevitably surface at the most unlikely moment and cause greater distress, not only to ourselves but to others too. Freedom comes when we confront ourselves in truth, with no masks, no pretence, and no performance. Freedom comes when we expose the lies we have led others to believe and we boldly admit that this is who we really are. How buried are your emotions? Find someone that you trust to talk to. Dare, to be honest, and let that freedom flow. In truth, there is always help available, but we cannot receive it if we choose to live a lie. No one can be helped unless they first admit there is a problem!

As his emotions subsided, we discussed the possibilities ahead, and a joy returned as we continued on our journey. Today was my grandson's third birthday, and he was about to have an unexpected guest to his celebrations, as they had not told the children that I was coming.

As we pulled up outside the front veranda, the door was flung open by two very excited grandchildren; five-year-old Megan and her brother Michael, the birthday boy. Both were calling out excitedly to their father in their native tongue, saying something like, "It is Michael's birthday, he has cake, he has presents!" As my son got out of the car they were jumping with joy that daddy was home.

I was sitting on the other side of the car, it was dark, they live in a rural area so the only visibility we had was the glow of the lights streaming from the lounge windows. I opened the car door, and as I stepped out and stood up, my head appeared above the roof of the car and the children were then able to see me. They came to a sudden halt in their celebrations, their eyes grew wide as they registered who I was, then Megan spoke in a tone of such affection, but almost in disbelief:"Farmor?"

They watched as I walked round from the other side of the car totally unaided by their father. As I walked towards them, they slowly backed away from me into the house and sought the reassurance of their mum that everything was okay. I walked up the three steps onto the veranda and approached the doorway. I was choked in tears, I extended my arms towards her, and Megan ran to me, throwing herself into my body, wrapping her arms around my hips. I bent down and picked her up, for the first time ever while standing up. She wrapped her arms tightly around my neck, her legs around my waist, and in the most intimate whisper repeated over and over again, with such tenderness into my ear, "Farmor, Farmor, Farmor,"

I sobbed as I was able to stand and hold my first born grandchild confidently in my arms, and we had that moment of intimacy that no one else can intrude on. A moment treasured forever! I held her for some time, until she loosened her grip, pulled her head off my shoulder and I smiled and kissed her on the cheek. As she unwrapped her legs from around me, I gently lowered her to the ground.

Michael was standing watching from a distance, close to his mother's side for reassurance. He had always been the more reserved of the two children, especially around 'strangers,' until he felt safe. I held out my arms to invite him towards me, half expecting that he wouldn't respond. In a moment, he let go of his mum's hand and ran towards me with a beaming grin of acceptance, and as I confidently scooped him up into my arms, he too just nuzzled into my neck, arms holding me tight, and as I swayed left to right in a gentle rocking motion in my tears, he just relaxed and surrendered into the moment.

I was aware of their parents tearfully observing. Then my son commented to Lindsey, "You don't seem surprised that Mum is walking. Did you know?" Lindsey stepped forward to give me her own welcoming embrace, as I asked him to forgive her for keeping it from him. He smiled, and agreed, that for him, to see it first for himself was the most amazing time ever!

As we had dinner, presents, and cake to celebrate Michael's third birthday, it was a joy to be with them on his special day, instead of observing from a distance. Those few days with the family were so different from any other trip I had ever taken to visit them. I could walk around the home with the children, freely going up and down their stairs, and played games on the floor together. We went shopping, walked around the supermarket pushing the trolley together, and I watched Megan at her horse riding lesson before going to a Christmas Fair. The children were just as much amused about hearing the sound of my voice again, as well as my freedom to pretend to chase them or sit on the floor with them. I am so incredibly blessed to have been able to celebrate in this way.

> ......weeping may stay for the night,
> but rejoicing comes in the morning.
>
> **Psalm 30:5**

Every tragedy, every difficult circumstance that we go through, can bring us to our knees, and in the first instance, as we go through the emotional and physical pain, it is easy to believe that we will never get through it. Yet, moment by moment, day by day, as we face ourselves, our emotions, the detail, the devastation, the possible changes to our lives, there are choices to be made. We are stronger than we think, and when we lay down our expectations and deal with the issues as they actually are, and not as we imagine them to be, our disappointment fades and we begin to realise that there is always a way forward. There may be tears in the dark night of the suffering, but contrary to first belief, it will not stay like that forever. One day the joy will return, freedom will come, and we will be thankful for all that we are, and all that we have, despite all things.

> **[5] If any of you lacks wisdom, you should ask God, who gives generously to all without finding fault, and it will be given to you.**
>
> **James 1:5**

Nobody is perfect; no one person has all the answers. When we do not know what to do we can make rash decisions and blunder from one disaster to another. I have learned to include God in everything, I talk to Him, and I expect Him to show me what I should do. God speaks in many ways, often through conversations with other people who have no idea what I am going through, but something they say resonates in my spirit as an action to take for myself. The Bible is the Word of God, the source of all wisdom into every situation of life. Then there is the 'knowing' that just sits in my understanding and leads me by peace into what I should do.

We are not meant to live as an 'island' isolated away from each other. We are called to be relational. We need each other! Having good friends or family that we can talk to without fear of judgement or criticism is so important. It isn't that those people necessarily have the answers, but as we talk things out, we can hear our own words and perhaps begin to realise the truth of how we really feel about things as we speak. We are then able to see things more clearly for ourselves and understand in a better way what we have to do.

If we are not prepared to face the truth of how we feel, we remain in a prison, trapped in the circumstances. The moment we can speak it out, to admit that we have a problem, we are then able to confront in truth, we have then taken the first step to victory and freedom to claim a better future. Anything hidden traps us into bondage, we live in lies and deception, but the only one we are deceiving is ourselves.

It is so easy to think that the problem is yours, it is hidden, and no one else can possibly know what is going on, or even care about you. That is never the case. People are more astute than you think. Trust those close to you, and don't be surprised when they admit they have seen the problem for themselves and they have been wanting to help you, but they didn't know how. But now, by including them, you enable them to be the help that you need and you realise you are never alone, and just how much you are loved.

I am eternally thankful to God for every person He brought to surround me in the difficulty of my circumstances, to love me, to help me, to sacrifice in so many ways for me. They were the 'hand', the 'ears', the 'heart', the 'eyes', the 'voice', and the 'embrace 'of Jesus into my life in every situation. My victory is assured because of who God is, and who I allow Him to be to me and for me. I encourage you to consider doing the same.

> Yet the Lord longs to be gracious to you;
> therefore he will rise up to show you compassion.
> For the Lord is a God of justice.
> Blessed are all who wait for him!
>
> **Isaiah 30:18**

God longs to show His grace to you, if included in your life He will show you grace and compassion. There is nothing you can do to make Him love you more; there is nothing you can do to make Him love you less. He is love. Pure sacrificial love.

23 | Moving Forward

As I write this chapter, it has now been five hundred and twenty days, or one year, five months and three days since my body was healed by Jesus.

Life has become so different. I am free!

I have been free to enjoy my family in a whole new way. I can join my adult children out for meals without consideration for a wheelchair space, and partake in group conversations and laughter without feeling numb and 'spaced out' on medication. When I was ill, my son often thought that I was 'low' or 'moody', but I wasn't, I just couldn't concentrate or focus when in a group scenario, where lots of people were talking and laughing together. Fatigue took over and I would close down.

I can now take the grandchildren to the park on my own. I can push them on the swings, the roundabouts and the zip wire, play ball and watch them on their bikes or scooter at the skate park.

Meeting friends outside the home has brought connectivity to a whole new group of people in many different settings. Variety has certainly become a way of life. But I have also had to ask for their understanding as I take time out to write this, and many other books and articles to come.

The radical change in my physical capacity also brought a far-reaching effect on my finances. I have been so thankful for the welfare support system that supported me through my frailty, but, on being healed, I was no longer able to claim those benefits. I could not afford to remain living in my own home, and so, yet again, I have had to move.

God's provision is always perfect, but I could not have pre-empted how He would work this one out!

My son and his wife both work full time and, as their jobs create more demand, they require more help with their children. As they were considering employing a full-time, live-in nanny, they decided to offer me the chance to help out with the grandchildren instead. I am reciprocated with a roof over my head and a chance to re-evaluate where my life is heading. I know this is only for a season, because new doors of opportunity will continue to open as I step into all that my life will be now, and if I need a place of my own at some time again in the future, I am confident that God will provide.

The family also have their own quality time without me having to be around, as I have respite at Esther's house to focus on my writing. Another miracle after the history of events between us!

Helping with the grandchildren has been a real joy and part of my continued recovery. Walking the children to and from school has enabled me to experience many new firsts:

Exercise – twice daily to school and back. Regular walking has increased my stamina and muscle strength.

- Walking in the early morning sunshine is such a joy, to feel the warmth of the sun on my face and body is amazing.

- Walking in the early morning frost is exhilarating as I feel the crisp autumn leaves crunch beneath my feet.

- Walking in the soft snow with frozen slushy ice underneath is a challenge to say the least. But I did it for the first time in years, and I didn't fall over!

- Walking in the rain feeling the raindrops on my head and running down my face is a joy to behold when I haven't been able to venture out in it for so many years.

So many of these everyday things are taken for granted and complained about often. There are many people living in restriction who would love to swap places with us if they could!

Then there are other aspects of life that I have learned to contend with again:

- I can go to the supermarket, wander around at my leisure, choose what I want from the shelf, put it in the shopping trolley, and when I get to the checkout I can unload it onto the conveyor belt and pack the bags myself. The first time I did this, I was just so excited, and other people in the queue just looked at me with curious confusion and a look of 'we have a right one here' on their faces. I was ecstatic as I was able to do for the first time what they take for granted to be able to do every day. I just wanted to dance with joy.

- In the summer it was even more freedom as I went back to the Lake District with Esther and her husband. This time there was no wheelchair needed, and I could leave the hostel whenever I wanted. For the first time ever, I walked around the lakes and up and down some of the hills on a low incline. It felt amazing, and this was only seven months after my body was healed. People who knew my history were amazed at the speed of my progress, and those who I met for the first time were so excited and encouraged by my story.

At one point, I even fell over as I came down an incline walking on loose gravel. I was trying to avoid a large cow pat, not looking where my feet were stepping, and I was mortified as I could feel myself falling, because I thought I might land in the middle of the smelly pile. I turned to the left in mid-air in my attempt to avoid it and landed heavily on my side. Victory all round – I missed the mess, and I didn't have any physical reaction to the fall!

This photograph was taken on my first ever incline walk, just seven months after my healing was completed.

Three weeks later I was able to go back and visit my son and the family in Europe. For the first time ever, I walked through the forest that runs alongside their home, picking berries with the grandchildren. I also posed on my son's motorbike, just for fun; I am not a biker chick at heart! Again, the freedom to roam, and to be able to rough and tumble with the family was a luxury after so many years of confinement.

I have had the privilege of doing local speaking events where I have been challenged and tested in my ability to speak for Jesus. It is not something that I naturally align myself with, but in the power of the Holy Spirit, I can do whatever God leads me into. After all, it is not about me, it is all about Him!

As I write this, I am reminded that in 2012 I was asked to speak briefly at a women's conference. I was surprised by the invitation as I had never done anything like it before. It was a real challenge, but I knew it was the right thing to do. The prospect of speaking in front of a large group of people was not a comfortable position to be in for someone who was so physically frail and confined to an electric wheelchair.

But then I was encouraged in an amazing way when I listened to a podcast, by an Australian evangelist and speaker, called Nick Vujicic. He explained that he knew that God was calling him to speak around the world, but he questioned how he could possibly go and do that, as he was born without arms and legs!

God told him to write down the words, GO DISABLED, and then to underscore the letters in a particular way. As he did so, he read 'GOD IS ABLED.'

I knew immediately that the invitation was from God, and that if I would 'GO' to the conference while 'DISABLED', my GOD IS ABLED!

As I was sitting in my wheelchair in front of approximately two hundred and fifty women, God enabled me to speak. At one point I was led to say, "As you look at me and see my wheelchair, you see me as 'disabled'. My disability is obvious to you, but this wheelchair is not my identity.

However, as I look at you, every one of you is disabled too; you just don't know it. You have been damaged by broken relationships, in marriage, in friendship, in family. You have broken dreams, financial restrictions, loss of jobs and emotional and physical sickness. But because you don't need a wheelchair, or any other physical aid to support you, your disability is 'hidden' to the outside world and you think you are keeping it secret. But God knows everything about you, and He loves you, and He wants to help you. Your circumstances are not your identity!"

This is true for every one of us. But what will we choose to do about it? Only when confronted in truth, will we receive the help that we need, and overcome the difficulties. God will help us if we will let Him.

In 2016, after being healed, I had the privilege of speaking in a prison. It was one of the most exciting moments in my speaking adventures so far. As I shared the details of my journey, they all responded with such excitement as they clapped and cheered at what they were seeing and hearing about the power of God. I was able to encourage them, that whatever the circumstances of their life, whatever the confines of their situation, whatever they had brought upon themselves by their choices, Jesus still loved them and wanted to set them free. They may be physically restricted, but their heart could be as free as they chose it to be.

They could live in a prison cell, but they could still be free in their spirit. They could learn from the situation, be transformed and changed by it and be over-comers despite all things, or they could live in denial of their responsibility and live feeling trapped. Jesus loves them and he wants to set them free. Their reaction was incredible. Some of those prisoners are freer in themselves than many people who live on the outside of the prison walls. They looked, they saw, they understood and they responded to the love and power of Jesus!

Since then, I have also travelled to the United States and to Canada, where I have had the opportunity to share the testimony of my life to encourage many other people of the power of God that is available to each and every one of us.

And then, there is this book. As I have surrendered to write, the memories have all come flooding back in such detail, and I have relived every moment of the twelve years as though it was happening now. I am overwhelmed by my emotions and so humbled by the grace of God in my life, and His divine power.

Going through the suffering for twelve years was a challenge, but I never cried out to God to ask, "Why me?"

Why not me? I am not excluded from adversity just because I follow Jesus. In fact, the Bible is very clear that we WILL go through adversity.

Although the Lord gives you the bread of adversity and the water of affliction, your teachers will be hidden no more; with your own eyes you will see them

Isaiah 30:20

But it also promises that we are never alone, God is always with us, and He will carry us through and teach us many things through it all. He is our comfort, our strength, our provider, our encourager, our teacher, and He has a plan to lead us into victory.

The Lord himself goes before you and will be with you; he will never leave you nor forsake you. Do not be afraid; do not be discouraged.

Deuteronomy 31:8

**Even though I walk through the darkest valley, I will
fear no evil, for you are with me; your rod and your staff,
they comfort me.**

Psalm 23:4

But I know that when faced with any life altering struggle or loss, many people do ask:

"Where is God?"

"Why would God let this happen to me?"

It is good to ask these questions, and we cannot live in
denial of our circumstances. The Bible is filled with stories
of God's strongest followers overcoming some of their life's
greatest battles. Joseph, Paul, and David are just a few, and
they are worth looking into so that you can understand
more about them. All I can say is, I learned to hold onto
Jesus even though, at times I could not 'feel' Him, and He
brought me through every single time.

I do not question His sovereignty (supreme power or
authority), I do not doubt His presence even if I cannot
'feel' Him, and I know that out of the mess of my life, there
is a message to encourage other people. God will turn this
around for good in my life and for His glory!

In 2005 I read this Bible text:

As he went along, he saw a man blind from birth. His
disciples asked him, 'Rabbi, who sinned, this man or his
parents, that he was born blind?'

'Neither this man nor his parents sinned,' said Jesus,
**'but this happened so that the works of God might be
displayed in him.**

John 9:1-3

God has truly displayed His works in my life. He wants
to do the same in your life too. Will you let Him? Talk to

God in prayer, ask someone to pray with you, be transparent in how you feel and, as you look to Him for help, see His answers come.

24

God's Timing is Perfect

As I went from strength to strength in my physical capacity, I had to complete final appointments with hospital consultants. I had been under the pain management clinic for eight years so they knew me well. They, like my doctor, were amazed at the physical transformation in my body. There were tears of disbelief and joy at what they were now seeing. Again, they could not understand how, and they had never seen such a radical change in someone's situation as they could see now, but they could not deny what they were looking at.

As they discharged me from their clinic, they wrote to my doctor to advise that I no longer needed their help. I had received treatment from them since 2007, but today, I had been seen at their clinic and I was fully recovered. I had told them that 'God' had done this!

My time of sickness could be counted in many ways – four thousand, two hundred and ten days, or six hundred and one weeks and three days, or eleven years, six months and nine days.

Whichever way it is measured, it was a time of intense physical suffering, restriction, and frailty; it was beyond measure in the diverse emotional distress. The practical losses of my job, finances, homes and friendships were life changing.

However, it was a time of radical spiritual transformation that turned my life upside down, inside out and back to front for Jesus. The intimacy of His heart that bled into mine with such awe inspiring love, hope, truth and radical freedom, despite the circumstances, was immeasurable.

Our choices affect us, but they affect other people too. I look back now at the first diagnosis of 'whiplash' and the predicted two weeks I would have to take off from work – my choice in that first instance to spend my time with God was a decision that was to become life changing. It flowed into seven months, and then into seven years isolated away, going deeper in my understanding of who God is, who He wants to be to me, to you, to everybody.

Then, over the next five years, that intimacy would flood out into the lives of so many people as God caused our paths to cross. His love washed over so many people and transformed their lives too.

In early 2005 I remember reading a story in the Bible about a woman who was sick for twelve years, who had spent all of her money on seeking a cure through doctors but without success. But then, as she reached out and touched the hem of Jesus' garment, she was healed. I came across the same story many times over the years and I used to casually consider, 'surely God is not saying it will be twelve years before I will become well again?' but then, as quickly as the thought entered my head, it would go.

But yes, I was healed in the twelfth year of my sickness. During those twelve years, I learned how to draw so close to Jesus - I was able to reach out and touch Him, in heart to heart intimacy - and I was touched by Him in His healing grace, through obedience to take Holy Communion as He directed. I cannot help but be overwhelmed in tears as I write. How intimate is our God! And not just for me, but He wants to be the same for you too.

> So Jesus went with him.
> A large crowd followed and pressed round him. [25] And a woman was there who had been subject to bleeding for twelve years. [26] She had suffered a great deal under the care of many doctors and had spent all she had, yet instead of getting better she grew worse. [27] When she heard about Jesus, she came up behind him in the crowd and touched his cloak, [28] because she thought, 'If I just touch his clothes, I will be healed.' [29] Immediately her bleeding stopped and she felt in her body that she was freed from her suffering.
> [30] At once Jesus realised that power had gone out from him. He turned round in the crowd and asked, 'Who touched my clothes?'
> [31] 'You see the people crowding against you,' his disciples answered, 'and yet you can ask, "Who touched me?"'
> [32] But Jesus kept looking around to see who had done it. [33] Then the woman, knowing what had happened to her, came and fell at his feet and, trembling with fear, told him the whole truth. [34] He said to her, 'Daughter, your faith has healed you. Go in peace and be freed from your suffering.'
>
> Mark 5:24-34

As I have picked up the thread of my life and come out of being 'cared for' and taken up 'independent' living again, it has been a time of many overwhelming emotions. To see so many different reactions in other people as they observe what has happened to me has at times been incredulous.

Because we are all so unique and individually made, Christians are no different to anybody else. They come in many different aspects of belief and experience in their faith journey; therefore, they respond in such individual ways. Many have been overwhelmed, so elated, and so encouraged to believe for God to do so much more in their lives because of what they have seen Him do in mine. For some, human logic gets in the way: they cannot explain it, so can they believe it? Others have been praying for my healing for years and cannot deny what they are now seeing, but are baffled by God's way of answering their prayers.

In our faith journey, our belief has to come not from what we understand with our brain, with human logic and problem sorting, but it has to come from what we know to be true in our hearts. We have to let the truth drop eighteen inches down from our head to our heart if we are to truly surrender and believe by faith!

The people who were closest to me on my journey, especially those who were in the Bible study groups that I fell into leading, continue to love and accept me for who I am, and they are watching expectantly as God continues to do what only He can do to take my life forward from here.

But there are some who have stepped away in fear and confusion in what they do not understand, not knowing how to relate to me anymore now that I am well. The help that they used to give, when I was so frail, was now no longer needed. So to them, it seemed that they were no longer needed either.

I can understand how they might feel, but it is so important that each one of those people would understand their self-worth. As much as I appreciated all the help that they gave, for which I will be eternally grateful, what is more precious, and has always been more important to me, is the heart to heart connection that we have in friendship. Who they are as a person, has always been far more important to me, than anything that they did. Those friendships are special and purposed and part of my life's journey!

While I was ill I was always at home if people wanted to pop in, or on the other end of the telephone if they needed to talk. Now I am able to go out and about and my world has become bigger and more diverse. Though I would love for people to continue the journey with me, and to experience more of what God wants to do, they have a free will choice, and sadly, not everyone has chosen to stay in place to enjoy the moment.

If we approach God with human logic and understanding then we will miss the diverse power and beauty of who God is.

There are also many people that were aware of my situation who do not go to church, including my neighbours in the apartment complex of over a hundred dwellings. What a joy it has been and so many tears have been shared, as they have met me outside my home and suddenly recognised me, realised I am walking and talking, and they have wanted to know how? They accepted the simplicity of the truth shared, and freely celebrated with me, and some have accepted Jesus and begun a whole new journey for themselves.

Now faith is confidence in what we hope for and assurance about what we do not see.
Hebrews 11:1

Definition of **Faith**:
Complete trust or confidence in someone or something
Strong belief in doctrine, based on spiritual conviction rather than proof

Faith is a very personal journey. Not everyone is called to endure what I have been through. Going through it was painful, traumatic, testing, challenging, life changing and, at times, almost cost me my life. Would I have chosen to go through it if I had known about it before the event?

NO!

Who would choose to?

But having been taken through it by faith, I can honestly say, I wouldn't swap one second of the learning curve that I have taken in Jesus. I am who I am today because of who He is, and all that He wants to be in my life, and in my future. He has equipped and trained me up in the way that I should go.

As previously shared, God has used butterflies so many times to get my attention and to speak to me. As I look back over this journey, I liken it to the analogy of a caterpillar becoming a butterfly.

God accepted me just as I was, at a point when I was frail, damaged and hurting from the effects of my life journey thus far. I wasn't exactly beautiful in the eyes of the world, just as a caterpillar may not look very attractive at first glance. In the early days of its existence, the caterpillar seemingly eats everything in sight and grows and grows. Then, one day, the caterpillar stops eating, hangs upside down from a twig or a leaf, and spins itself a silky cocoon. Hidden away in its protective casing, the caterpillar radically transforms its body, and eventually, after a physical struggle to do so, it emerges as a beautiful butterfly. It has wings to soar.

Over the years, I had fed on and absorbed the lies that the world, and my choices - good and bad – had thrown at me. But God had a plan. My injury took me aside into a 'cocooned' environment. As I turned to Him, God transformed me from the inside out, and I transitioned through a time of emotional, physical and spiritual healing, to become all that I am today. At the right time, I received my healing and I was released from the cocoon to emerge in my true identity. God has given me my freedom, I have wings, and I will soar in Him!

In 2009, God told me that 'He didn't need me to glorify Him!'

As I have shared my heart through this book, I truly believe that God has done that for Himself!

I will spend the rest of my life in witness for Jesus.

I have been ... RELEASED TO **ROAR**'.

Yet he did not waver through unbelief regarding the promise of God, but was strengthened in his faith and gave glory to God, [21] being fully persuaded that God had power to do what he had promised.

Romans 4:20-21

And the God of all grace, who called you to his eternal glory in Christ, after you have suffered a little while, will himself restore you and make you strong, firm and steadfast.

1 Peter 5:10

Now to him who is able to do immeasurably more than all we ask or imagine, according to his power that is at work within us, [21] to him be glory in the church and in Christ Jesus throughout all generations, for ever and ever! Amen.

Ephesians 3:20-21

To God Be The Glory!

Amen.

Appendix A

Witnesses

One of the blessings that I encountered while going through the difficulties of this experience was the number of people that crossed my path. There were so many medical professionals, personal care workers, and many new neighbours each time I had to move home. There were many new friendships through church and the Bible study groups that I had the privilege to be part of, and many others that were 'chance' encounters along the way.

So many people saw me go through the frailty, witnessed the transformation change in my miracle release, and they would like to share some of their own observations of the journey.

It is with humility and in sheer awe of God that I therefore include a small collection of eye witness accounts written in their own words, from people who have journeyed some of my moments through the years:-

Jackie B

To say that I witnessed a healing miracle over a period of 40 days seems far-fetched, but it is true!

I had seen Grace in some dark days when she was struggling with indescribable pain, unable to move, or be touched. But God had promised He would heal her, and she believed Him, and she hung on, not knowing how, when or where it would happen.

During the time when Grace was more or less housebound – except when others helped with the wheelchair, access into lifts, opening doors etc - she always welcomed people into her home and chatted, prayed, mentored and loved them. They went away having had a most precious and edifying time, knowing that Jesus had been the unseen guest.

About three weeks into her journey of decreasing her medication in obedience to God, I suddenly became aware that this gradual healing had started. Each week, I was aware of the changes taking place in Grace's body – more mobility coming from the pain easing - which brought about energy and a sharper mind, with a 'glad to be alive' appearance in her eyes!

It has been wonderful to know Grace, and I have been encouraged, taught, prayed for, loved and blessed by her, including enjoying lots of laughter together. I know it has all been from God, we are true sisters in Christ and best friends.

To have witnessed her healing has been a privilege, and I thank and praise the Lord, and I look forward to hearing and seeing how He will continue to work through her, as she lives for Him in this new phase of her life – an adventure in every sense of the word!

Thanksgiving
I give thanks to my God always for you because of the grace of God that was given you in Christ Jesus,
1 Corinthians 1:4

Rachel W

I met Grace when she started attending my church in January 2011. For a few weeks, I just watched her and was amazed at her joy and peace, as she was in a wheelchair. Eventually, I introduced myself to her and I asked about her situation. She explained about the car accident, which I identified with, having had an accident myself the previous year that resulted in me suffering from depression.

Grace offered to pray for me and gave me her phone number to arrange a time. This took me by surprise as she was a complete stranger to me. I arranged what was to be the first of many times that I would visit her in her home, where I would receive prayer, help, and support as she spoke truths about my life that needed to change. It was clear that she had a God-given understanding for me.

I was able to talk to Grace about anything, and she listened without judgement. God changed my life for the better. I am now completely off anti-depressant tablets, and I have so much joy, confidence, and better self-esteem. This Bible verse, in particular, encouraged and helped me:

I can do all things through Christ, because He gives me strength.

Philippians 4:13

During this time, Grace used elbow crutches to walk indoors and needed someone to take her outdoors in a wheelchair. She never once complained about her situation and was always mindful of others. I must add that she always believed that God would heal her.

Sadly, I was aware of a gradual deterioration in her health - less mobility, chronic fatigue, more pain – and eventually she had to use an electric wheelchair indoors, and outside her home. She also needed the help of carers.

Her voice began to fail and she tried various methods of amplification. But, during this time, she continued to lead the Monday night Bible study group in her home. This was a great source of teaching and encouragement to myself and others, as we have learned more about God and the Bible, and how to apply the truth to our lives. Grace regularly attended church and other activities, despite her frailty, and led our group to arrange many outreach events for the local neighbourhood. I remember her organising a barn dance - and she really enjoyed watching other people having fun – although she was restricted to a wheelchair.

In November 2015 I was in Tenerife on a family holiday, and the day before returning home I received a text message from Grace to say that she could not wait to catch up with me. She then shared the good news that she had received her healing! I did not sleep that night with excitement, and could not wait to get home and see her. Consequently, I was on her doorstep as soon as I returned! It was such a thrill to hear her voice speaking so clearly and to see her walking around and able to dance! Grace is now free from all the restrictions and pain, able to go wherever she wants to, no longer needing a wheelchair! She has been invited to share her story with many different groups and has travelled to different parts of the world to do so. I am so grateful that God brought Grace into my life. What a blessing she is to me and many others. One particular thing that Grace taught me is:

You have to 'do' something different – to 'have' something different.

You cannot keep doing the same thing over and over again, and then expect the outcome to be different!

Tracy N

My journey with Grace began back in 2011 whilst I was working as a care assistant and I was assigned to her personal care, supporting her with basic care needs. As I got to know her, I got the opportunity to learn more about her situation. I was filled with deep compassion as Grace went on to unfold the events that led to her circumstance of physical disability. However, what struck me was her inner strength. She always had a positive outlook on her life. Every time I would visit Grace, she always had a lovely smile, a radiant countenance and a sense of peace. I soon learned that she was a Christian just like me, which was wonderful to know.

Although Grace was in a difficult situation physically, as she was constantly in pain, she never seized to talk about the goodness of God and she believed with all her heart that God was going to heal her body, as he had promised. This woman of God had unwavering faith. I remember we often prayed together, and she became an inspiration and an encourager to me. In 2012, I moved on to a different job, which meant that I was not able to see Grace very often.

In January 2016, Grace contacted me to inform me that she had been completely healed, and was therefore inviting me to an evening of worship at her local church where she would be sharing her testimony. I was filled with joy and excitement at what the Lord had done and I would not have missed that service! When I saw Grace at the worship service, standing on her own two feet with strength and stamina, for a moment it felt like a dream. I had only ever seen her in an electric wheelchair. She stood in front of the congregation and shared her testimony. What a night it was, as we all joined her to worship God for his amazing love and mercy.

For me, Grace's story is one of someone who has stood patiently on God's promise. She has been patient to see the manifestation of God's promise for her life. That is serious unwavering faith. This great woman of God is an inspiration to me and many Christians on hearing God, obeying God and standing on his Word. To God be the glory forever and ever!!!!!"

Diane H

I first met Grace in 2007 at the hospital pain clinic. We were both on a course to learn how to live with chronic pain for life, as there is no cure. My group had dropped to just two of us, so they asked the group that Grace was in if we could join them. There was only two weeks left which meant they had all bonded in her group. At that time Grace was on crutches and her walking was unsteady. When the course finished Grace invited the entire group to her home for lunch. This was very nice. Then we went once a week to see her. Gradually everyone else stopped going apart from me.

As our friendship grew over the years, Grace's health deteriorated, slowly at first, then she got worse very fast and ended up in a wheelchair, unable to go out without someone with her. Not only did she lose her mobility, she also lost her voice and could only speak in a whisper. So then I used to do most of the talking!

Throughout it all Grace stayed strong, and always said that one day God would heal her. We would often talk about God, even though I had lost my faith many years before. And I also told her that I didn't believe in God. One day when I went to see Grace she said, "Can I show you something? so naturally I said 'yes'. She then got up from her chair and walked across the room and back. Then she said, "I can dance" and did a little wiggle, and as she spoke I then realised that her voice had come back.

I was amazed, but all I could say was 'you're so tall'. Which she was, but it was the first time I'd seen her standing up straight. I agreed it was a miracle but was reluctant to admit that God had done it. But God had a plan when he brought Grace into my life, which I didn't know at that time. After being invited to various things at the church, I eventually agreed to go to something. When asked if I went to church, I always replied 'I don't do churchy things' After a while, I was invited to do the Alpha course, even if it was just for the food! I went but the whole time I still said I hadn't changed my opinion.

Then I was invited to the discipleship group to learn about the new testament, and I agreed to go. I was still not changing my mind, until one week when we were reading about the Transfiguration, and it was then that God spoke to me. He helped me to remember a dream that I had had when I had believed in God many years before. I had the same dream many times. I saw a garden with lots of different coloured trees that looked like candy floss. The colours were so radiant and more beautiful than anything I'd ever seen before, and I always felt so at peace and happy there. It felt like I'd been shown a small piece of Heaven.

When I next saw Grace we were sat in the garden of her old house, where I first started seeing her many years ago, and I told her what had happened. She then asked me if I believed in God now. To which I said, "Yes, I did." So she asked me if I wanted to say the prayer to accept God back into my life. I thought about it for a couple of minutes and then said "Yes, lets do this" So I repeated the prayer after Grace.

So yes, God did perform a miracle by healing Grace, and also guided me back to Him through her. It only took me nine years! Now I see a truly strong, happy and healthy woman in Grace, doing God's work, and I feel truly blessed that God brought her into my life, and to call her my friend. It's been an incredible journey. Thank you, God.

Sue W

I first met Grace when she came to Westcliff Baptist Church in 2011. She was in a wheelchair.

She invited people to her home to listen to tapes by Joyce Meyer. I found this very inspiring and helpful. Grace also gave us good teaching from the Bible, and a number of us regularly met every Monday evening at her home.

Grace often spoke of her recovery that would come, as she always believed that Jesus would heal her. As her condition worsened and her voice disappeared, she became so ill that I felt that her healing would be in Heaven, rather than on earth.

It has been so wonderful to see the miraculous healing of a good friend and to know that God is always with us.

Jean B

I first met Grace one Sunday morning when she was wheeled in her wheelchair into our church. She had no idea how she was going to get back home as her friend had to leave her on her own. I immediately offered to help, and there started a great friendship, which I am so thankful to God for.

In time, Grace started a Monday night group for Bible Study. Because of her physical limitations, she needed help to set practical things out like refreshments and seating. I offered to help, and we used to pray together before everyone else arrived. Over the coming months and years that followed, I saw Grace get weaker and weaker in her body, but her love for Jesus and the group never faltered. Some nights I would arrive and find her in so much pain and fatigue that I would advise her to cancel the evening. But she always refused, insisting that God would give her the strength that she needed to carry on. As we prayed together, God was true to His word as she claimed it over herself, and I would watch her come alive as she was given the strength to carry on.

At the end of the evening, she would sit in her chair to gather her strength, so I could help her into her night clothes and make sure she was ready for getting into bed. I would look at her and see the pain in her eyes and would pray desperately that God would heal her. As our friendship grew I wanted to help her more. So as she became frailer, and I realised that standing up, walking, showering and getting dressed was becoming more of a problem, I was led to offer my help.

The first morning I helped I knew it was difficult for her because she was losing her independence more and more. I knelt on the floor to dry her feet, and as I took her foot into the towel she suddenly began to sob. As she cried, I thought I had been too rough and caused her pain, because I knew that she was so sensitive to touch. But as she pulled herself together, she explained that as she was watching what I was doing, she had seen Jesus drying her feet, just as He did with the disciples.

As Grace got weaker she had to have professional carers to look after her, to give her the help that she needed, which was more than I could do for her. This was very hard for Grace to accept, but she gave in very gracefully because she knew that was what God wanted her to do. She was a wonderful witness to me through this time because she never took her eyes off Jesus, and always had time to talk and to pray with me when I had problems, always pointing me back to God, to trust Him for everything.

It was on one of these visits, just before the end of the 40 days, that I saw a change taking place and Grace shared with me that God was healing her. As she walked across the room and bent over to touch her toes, I was speechless and just wanted to cry. It really was a 'WOW' moment. Her voice was still a whisper, but the strength in her legs was amazing. I am so thankful to God for the privilege of witnessing such a miracle! It has really blown my mind, and I am encouraged that what God has done for Grace, He can do for anyone else who believes. My faith has grown big time as I have watched and listened to Grace's journey with Jesus, and I am so excited for what the future holds for both of us, as our friendship continues, and we journey together in Him.

Verity B

One Sunday morning back in 2011, a lady in a wheelchair landed in our church, and that proved to be the start of an amazing journey into yet untapped territory for me. At the time, I, being a reticent type, held back, but I was avidly listening to all the questions being asked by other people each time we saw her. The one I remember most was, "Do you do small group Bible studies? We already had an established small group, but without leadership, and at that point, we were about to fold, so when this visitor eventually told us some weeks later that she had, in fact, led a study group, we immediately jumped at the opportunity to get to know her more!

This lady was called Grace, and she had recently moved into a flat next to the church. She had noticed a street sign leading to us. A friend had dropped her off that first morning but was unable to stay, so Grace was at our mercy!

We soon learned that Grace had been in a car accident, and her mobility was impaired, so she was pretty much housebound without assistance. This resulted in a small group of us meeting in her flat on a Friday morning, and boy, were we in for a big surprise as we began to learn more about Grace and her amazing journey with God!

Not only was Grace an excellent Bible teacher, but she was an incredible witness to the power of God. This was so new and refreshing to us all, to hear about her deep faith and personal witness to a God she clearly believed would one day heal her. How could she know? What did she possess that none of us had?

Each Friday morning as we continued to meet together, we knew that we too would come away knowing we had met with the Living God. Consequently, we began to make strides ourselves in discovering that this same God we had worshipped diligently for many years, could move amongst us and develop our gifts too, by the power of His Holy Spirit.

Our group acquired the name 'Butterflies' due to the significance of these beautiful creatures in Grace's life. By this time we were all hungry for more of the vastness of God's love for us and the equipping for ministries of our own.

In the early days it became apparent that I felt a real bond with Grace, and one Friday I remember particularly because I noticed her shuffling along inside her flat, holding onto the wall for support, her physical pain all too apparent. In that moment I was overwhelmed with compassion and overcome with emotion because I sensed a connectivity. This was when I realised this discernment was given for a purpose. What has always amazed me is how Grace has been able to minister to others whilst being in horrendous pain herself, yet remaining so positive with her words of encouragement. How could I give up when I had this powerful role model? Yet all through, it was always about Christ glorified and never about herself.

I believe the Lord was drawing us closer together in friendship, and this astounds me because we are two very different people. However, I recognised in Grace, gifts that would draw me closer to God. I had never understood that it was possible to be in a close and intimate relationship with an awesome God, so my eyes have truly been opened.

Ecclesiastes 4:9-12 is a passage that I was given which gives credence to this, especially the final sentence, 'A cord of three strands is not easily broken.'

> [9] Two are better than one,
> because they have a good return for their labor:
> [10] If either of them falls down,
> one can help the other up.
> But pity anyone who falls
> and has no one to help them up.
> [11] Also, if two lie down together, they will keep warm.
> But how can one keep warm alone?
> [12] Though one may be overpowered,
> two can defend themselves.
> A cord of three strands is not quickly broken.
>
> Ecclesiastes 4:9-12

There have however been times when our friendship has been tested, but I have learned through that, because God will have His way, for his ways are greater than our ways.

Soon, we were meeting regularly in our friendship to share details of our lives and become better acquainted. Sometimes, we would play Scrabble, and Grace nearly always beat me despite often feeling fatigued! Through many moments of laughter, tears, and chocolate, we shared the ups and downs of life, but in all of this Christ was always at the centre.

In early November 2015, I arrived at Grace's flat, as usual, to accompany her to church, but this particular morning was far from usual. As I was waiting in her lounge, Grace appeared from her bedroom and walked slowly and steadily along her hallway towards me without holding on to anything. I immediately commented on this because I thought I may have imagined it, but no, the long promised miracle was unfolding before my eyes. The realisation hit me, causing me to break into uncontrollable sobbing as it all sank in. After years of praying for Grace's healing, I had witnessed first-hand the work of God's healing power.

Church was a struggle that morning, considering what I had just witnessed, and the taste of what Grace had been able to share with me. However, I knew the time for sharing with others was not yet ripe, so I needed to contain myself! This particular morning our minister had chosen to call us to the front of the church to receive Holy Communion. I agreed to pick up the bread and wine for Grace, but I was delayed by someone wanting me to pray for them, so our Minister and another lady helped her instead.

Two weeks later the truth was finally revealed when Grace got up out of her wheelchair and walked unaided to the front of the church. It was remarkable, and what greater witness to the healing power of Jesus could there be? Ever since then, Grace has taken every opportunity to speak out her story of a "God who is good – ALL the time!" This would not have been possible unless her voice had been restored too, so now, there was no stopping her.

Since Grace's healing, I have had to make adjustments, because I have not been needed to help out in the same way as before. While she has had to take time out writing this book, it has been difficult not having her around. But, I know when Grace enters the next stage of her amazing journey in Jesus; our friendship will have survived, because it has all been part of Gods incredible plan. Grace is a 'one off' and a remarkable ambassador for our awesome God, but she is also my special friend.

Jeanette B

I first met Grace in January 2011, when she 'landed' (her own words) in my church. I went to welcome her as she was sitting in her wheelchair, and since that day we have become great friends.

Grace lived in a flat near the church and I often visited for coffee and a chat. In the beginning she could answer the door by walking slowly and holding onto the walls for support. However, when she went outside, it was always with another person pushing her in her wheelchair.

Whenever I visited, Grace always welcomed me with a warm smile, enquiring how I was. This was amazing as she was in great pain and she also suffered from fatigue. We had many wonderful conversations about life and about God. Grace's face glowed as she talked about what God had done, and was doing in her life, and she often said, "God is good all the time," and "God is going to heal me."

Over time, Grace's physical condition deteriorated. She could hardly move due to increased pain and fatigue and she needed the help of carers daily. Her faith never diminished, rather, it was the opposite. She continued to 'glow' in God's love. Her whole life was surrendered to God and his love poured through her into everyone that she met. We all loved her and visiting her was so special. Despite the intense pain she welcomed everyone with a hug.

Grace had words of wisdom for all situations, whether you called her day or night, and she overflowed with compassion. Her carers loved coming to her flat because she ministered to them too. Amazing Grace!!

It was so difficult to watch someone that you love and admire suffer so much. Yet, Grace never wanted pity, only friendship. The worst thing, as far as I was concerned, was that she started to lose her voice, which eventually became inaudible. Yet, she constantly repeated, in a whisper, "God is good – all the time," and "God is going to heal me." While in church one day, in November 2015, I turned around to see Grace suddenly standing up from her wheelchair and starting to take her coat off. I was horrified, my first thought was that she was going to fall over. I was about to go towards her and help, when she took a step forward. Then to my utter amazement she walked from the back of the church to the front. She took the microphone and spoke in a loud clear voice. I can't remember what she said, but I saw and heard God's miracle! God had given Grace her healing miracle, that she knew He had promised, and in which she had never doubted!

When I invite my friends and Grace to the coffee shop, it is always a delight to hear her share her story, and to watch the expressions on people's faces. Their eyes well up and they listen, absolutely enthralled. One of my dear friends gave her life to Jesus after one such occasion.

Many people I know are either disabled, suffering from cancer or have other serious illnesses. Many do not know Jesus. I have seen Grace's miracle and I know there is hope for them too.

Grace's life and faith have been an inspiration to me. God bless you Grace, as you continue your journey with God.

Ruth D

I first met Grace at the school gates when we collected our children from school. We both just got on so well together, and over the years we both learned to talk together for England! We talked about our faith and often prayed together.

I have known Grace for 30 years now, through the ups and downs of life, through troubles and pain, both emotionally and physically, as Grace's family went through many difficulties on the journey of life. Yet, Grace never wavered in her faith in Jesus and trust in God. I have had the privilege of witnessing and seeing the beauty that God has created out of the pain, difficulties, and trauma of her life.

I watched Grace deteriorate from the accident and never heard her complain. Even in her pain and tears from time to time, she could only focus on God's love for her and she always believed that He would bring her through the suffering. Day after day she listened to Christian teaching messages, and when I was able to visit we had some lovely discussions as we learned about biblical truths together. She always had time for people and she listened to their troubles, but she never focused on her own difficulties.

I suggested getting a second doctor's opinion to understand why she was deteriorating. When she eventually did so, she was none the wiser. I got frustrated with no answers as to 'why?', yet Grace didn't. She just received God's peace and knew that she was in the mystery of God's hands.

As she became more disabled, days out became more difficult and limited in what we could do together. I would take her out from time to time to watch the sea, or to go to a wildlife country park to enjoy creation, but we could only do this by sitting in the car. As we talked and prayed together, these simple times brought such pleasures to her. She learned in the simple everyday life that we take for granted, that there is always something to be grateful for and to thank God for.

Grace eventually gave in to having to use a wheelchair, which opened up a door to be able to do more in life. I was able to take her to the shops and visit family, who lived quite a distance away. After each trip out she would suffer for days afterward with such chronic pain and distress to her body, yet she would push through to do something different, to have the more of life.

To watch the kickback of these outings on her body was painful, yet she never complained. There were times when I wouldn't suggest doing things because of this, and when I told her so, she would tell me off. She would say, "please let me decide."

I could see that even while using a wheelchair she was in such pain. Every bump and dip in the pavements would vibrate into her body. Knowing this, when I took her out in the car, I would avoid the bumps and dips in the road. Grace would often tell me that I was driving 'like a drunk' and that I would get stopped by the police. We would laugh together as I came up with an explanation that I was carrying the King's daughter.

As Grace's pain increased and also her disability, I began to lose sight of how I could help her, and I got lost in my own struggles of life, which sadly lead to a 5 year breakdown in our relationship, which added to her pain. Yet God never let her down in providing for all her needs.

We eventually reconciled (this is another story to be told). Looking back over those 5 years, Grace came through the pain of the breakdown in our friendship a richer person, both spiritually and in her character.

She prayed and patiently waited for God to break into my life, believing for me to come back through her front door. Even in all the pain of her body, and the pain that I caused her she never complained. When I did eventually go back, it was a shock to see how frail she had become, especially as she had no sound to her voice. She listened to me, and she chose to forgive me, and through the power of God's reconciliation, we became friends again. However, because of the breakdown, we are both so much closer to God, and stronger in our friendship in Christ, because of those 5 years.

Grace truly lives up to her God-given name "GRACE"

I am so grateful to the Lord for helping us to reconcile before he took Grace on her 40-day healing journey.

After a few months of reconciliation and catching up on each other's lives, we would regularly meet to worship and pray together. On one of these meetings, I arrived to find Grace in a really bad way. She was so wrecked in pain that she couldn't move from her reclined position in her chair, to sit up. I soon realised she wasn't in a very good place and I didn't want to leave her on her own.

In my Bible bag I had a book about Holy Communion, and as it was a short book, I asked if I could read it to her.

When I finished reading it, she brought herself up to a sitting position, saying, "I know, that I know, that I know, that for the next 40 days I have to take Holy Communion 3 times a day, and God is going to take me off the medication and heal me." I was shocked and didn't know where she had got that from while I was reading the book. We prayed about it together and I went home.

I stayed in touch, but when I rang her two days later, I knew something was seriously wrong! She was in a terrible state, so I dropped everything and went to her home. I found her in so much pain, and I was concerned that she was suicidal, as she didn't know what to do with herself. We talked it through. She confessed she had run ahead of God by stopping the tablets all at once. So we prayed together, and I left her in a place of peace, knowing she had agreed to take her tablets again.

From that moment, whenever I visited her, I could see physical changes taking place. There was lightness in her spirit and joy. Her face began to change. It was showing she wasn't in chronic pain. I saw her energy levels coming back and one day as we prayed together, I opened my eyes to find her on her knees and sobbing as she prayed. I was so delighted and in awe of what God was doing, that unknown to her, I took a picture of her with my phone.

One day she even offered to make the coffee, and then progressed to fixing lunch for me. I couldn't remember the last time she had done this. A few days later I suggested that we try the stairs up to her apartment. To my delight, she could do a few of them. It was getting so exciting day by day to see how God was healing her body. Every time I visited her I was in awe of God and wondered what new thing she would be able to do today. It was amazing to witness such changes, and yet be aware that many people didn't notice as God kept it hidden until she was fully healed.

Words cannot express my thankfulness to a loving Father God who brought me back into friendship with Grace and then allowed me to be part of her healing journey.

Thank you, Jesus, for healing Grace, all the glory belongs to you!

My Best Friend: Grace

"Wow! You've been best friends for 55 years? That's amazing!"

I've heard this response many times when I talk about my best friend Grace. We have been through thick and thin, tall and short (Grace is taller than me!) and laughter and tears over the years.

We met at school when we were five years old and we have remained the best of friends ever since, despite living in different parts of the country. We talk on the phone – a lot! My husband now knows that when we ring each other it will be a long chat, so he will duly put the kettle on and bring me a cup of tea!

I was happy when, despite her speech impediment, Grace achieved her long awaited ambition of joining the police force. She loved her job. She turned up at our old family home once in her uniform. That got the neighbours talking afterwards! It made me laugh, but I was proud to call her my best friend.

Over the years, as we both married, and Grace had her lovely family, I watched her raise her three children. We still saw each other when we could, and still had the endless phone calls sharing our lives. Gradually though, as the years passed, Grace started to become ill. I was concerned at first but confident the doctors would source the problem and she would get better.

But Grace didn't get better. She got worse. She had to give up her job. She had to give up her home and her driving too. Her symptoms became more profound and she became virtually housebound. Now I was extremely worried. Various trips to doctors and hospital consultants eluded no proper diagnosis. Some suggested it could be one thing, others suggested another. Her body was in extreme pain most of the time, amongst other symptoms that gradually appeared too. She was often on high doses of painkillers to try and relieve her discomfort. It came to the point where she had to have carers four times a day to help wash, dress and prepare meals for her. She also became wheelchair bound. I was devastated for her at this point.

We still talked when we could and often had Skype calls with each other. It was the one thing we could still do – talk! She would tire easily though and I often saw her just close her eyes and lay back in her chair assuring me that she was still listening to me talking, but that she needed to rest.

Despite all of this, the one constant she had in her life was her faith and belief in God. This grew stronger over the years and seemed to keep her going. It took her mind off all the problems and the immense pain in her body.

At Grace's worst, she became unable to speak. She lost her voice. For both of us that was the most devastating moment. It had been, until then, the one thing we could still do together. Before, we would chat, laugh and giggle uncontrollably for hours. Not now. It broke my heart. Yes, we could still text, email and message each other, but I couldn't hear my best friend's voice anymore. I cried a lot after that.

As we stayed in touch the best that we could, I knew that Grace's belief in God was growing stronger still. She had faith that sometime in the future God would heal her. I had doubts. However, I was not going to judge what she believed herself.

Then, the most amazing day of our friendship arrived. I remember it so clearly. It was a Sunday and the phone rang. My husband answered it, and after chatting momentarily came to find me and told me that Grace was on the phone. I said "What?!" I went to the phone to find my best friend able to talk to me again! In the next hour and a half of our conversation, she proceeded to blow me away with her story of how she had been healed by God, and step by step how it had happened. I sobbed through most of that conversation!

She also told me that in one of her earlier visits to her own doctor, she had told him that one day she believed she would be healed, and jokingly said she would dance with him in his surgery when that day arrived. Well, that day did arrive. She left me stunned when she told me that after her recovery, she had visited her doctor. He seemed utterly shocked to watch her walk into his room unaided and could hardly believe what he was hearing about how she was healed. What he did next still brings a lump to my throat every time I think of it – he stood up and asked her to dance right there in his surgery! He had remembered what she had once said.

The first time Grace and I met when she was well again was equally unbelievable. She walked towards me, perfectly normally. I could not believe my eyes, having seen her previously struggle to even stand. Yes, I cried again as we hugged each other.

I recently saw Grace at her surprise 60th birthday party last December. Her children had organised it in secret. She had no idea my husband and I were going to it. The look on her face when she eventually saw us both will stay with me forever. Yet again, as I watched her that night laughing, talking and thoroughly enjoying the friends and family around her, I found it overwhelming to understand and make sense of this healing process.

After twelve long years of illness, I can't pretend to understand what has actually happened to Grace. She no longer has any carers to help her and she doesn't use a wheelchair. There seems no logic to it all. Maybe there is no logical explanation. It is nothing short of a miracle!

All I know is...I now have my friend back, healthy and fully immersed in life again! Oh, and writing a book! And yes, we still do have those long giggly phone calls with each other. It's such a joy to hear her voice again. She's Grace - my amazing friend.

Yvonne F

Appendix B

Invitation

God has a plan for our brokenness. We are prone to keep looking for someone to love us, someone to care. But, we don't have to. God is love. God does care. He sees what we are going through, but sometimes, it is only as we go through storms, that we are reminded that HE is the one who we can lean on in times of trouble.

If you are experiencing hurt from broken relationships, or if you have been wounded from abuse in the past, or if you are grieving the loss of a loved one...whatever your pain is...then I encourage you to take shelter in the unconditional love of God.

The Lord is a refuge for the oppressed,
a stronghold in times of trouble.
Those who know your name trust in you,
for you, Lord, have never forsaken those who seek you.
Psalm 9:9-10

There is no one in your life who can bring comfort and healing like God can. He has such a deep love for you, shown through the sacrifice of His Son.

For God so loved the world that he gave his one and only Son, that whoever believes in him shall not perish but have eternal life.

John 3:16

His grace is all that we need and it is made perfect in our times of weakness.

But he said to me, "My grace is sufficient for you, for my power is made perfect in weakness." Therefore I will boast all the more gladly about my weaknesses, so that Christ's power may rest on me.

2 Corinthians 12:9

Thank you for allowing me to share my story with you. Whatever your faith values may have been before you read this book, I pray that my journey has perhaps made you think about, and begin to consider who God really is, and who He wants to be for you too.

Does He really love you? Would He accept you regardless of what you have done? Would He help you?

The resounding answer to all of these questions is 'YES!'

If you would like to begin your own journey with Jesus, if you would like to allow God to help you to live your life in freedom and peace despite your circumstances, if you would like to know that you are never alone and that you are always loved and accepted for who you are, then I would encourage you to talk to God.

Talking with God is called 'prayer.'

There is no set formula for us to follow to do this, or any special words. You can speak to Him anytime of the day or night, just as you would talk to a good friend. Simply tell God that you want to follow him, that you want to include Him in everything that you do.

When we know we have done something wrong, we can say 'sorry' to God, and be forgiven by Him. We can ask for Him to help us not to do that same wrong thing again.

We can say 'thank you' to Him for all the good things that happen to us every day.

When things are not going as we would like them to be, we can ask for His help.

It is all about relationship, and the best way to understand relationship with God is to have your own Bible, and read a little bit each day, asking God to help you to understand it.

It is good to tell someone that you trust, a good friend or your spouse/partner that you have decided to include God in your life.

Find a local church where you can meet with other people to be taught how to understand what the Bible says and to be encouraged in your new choices.

If you know that you want to do something, but you are not sure how to go forward from this point.

OR

If you would like to receive further encouragement, support and understanding in each of these matters, now that you have made a choice to include God in your life, then please contact Grace at:

gracertr17@gmail.com

Acknowledgements

Without the support and help of many people, this book would never have come into existence. I give my heartfelt thanks to:

My children: Unless I had been released from your expectations of me, to allow me to follow my heart, this would not have happened. Thank you!

My grandchildren: Their excitement and anticipation as they began to understand the concept of what I was aiming to do in writing this book was profound, and spurred me on, that the next generation would never forget who my Jesus is!

Ruth and Lynn: For 30 years of friendship, love, and support, in and through so many dramas. Thank you for listening to my heart's cry, my considerations, my doubts, and limitations. Thank you for every practical help, every conversation of encouragement, and for every prayer of faith. Thank you for the use of your home as a quiet haven to escape the world and focus on my God-given task, to write for His glory. Thank you for standing firm against the world, and not giving up on me!

Jean, Verity, Rachel, Sue, Jacky, Lindi, and Ruth, Ruth and Ruth, the mainstay of the Monday Group, and many others who have shared fellowship with us intermittently over the years. You were my training ground, my generous gift from God! Thank you for believing, trusting, and allowing me the privilege of seeing you being touched and transformed by Jesus over the years. Lifetime covenant friendships and our eternal future claimed together!

Jenny, a timely gift from God, compassionate and generous in heart, gentle in spirit and hungry for truth. Our journey continues for His glory.

Diane, so faithful in friendship through the pain, a journey into freedom for both of us was claimed! God's timing is always perfect!

John Western, Minister at Westcliff Baptist Church, my spiritual home. Thank you for your leadership, your discernment, your encouragement, and support, as I have journeyed through the circumstances into freedom. The church was privileged in witness, is challenged in faith and ever hopeful for the best that is yet to come! Thank you for believing in the future to which I am called. I am forever accountable in truth.

Emily Kate Chester, for your love, support, advice, wisdom, and encouragement as you proofread, and patiently edited the first 'read' of the raw manuscript. Our paths crossed again for 'such a time as this!' Thank you!

Ruth Dobson, my unofficial photographer, always alert in the most unlikely moments with her mobile phone. Evidence collector extraordinaire!

Chris at JETLAUNCH, for your incredible patience, outstanding support, and exceptional service. You are second to none! www.jetlaunch.net

Robert Roth for his sensitivity and interpretation as he completed the book cover design. Email: robert@amphetamedia.net

Kary Oberbrunner, the background support team, and all of the Igniting Souls Tribe at Author Academy Elite, without whom, this book would have remained a dream, and not become a reality! Thank you! You have taken me from the base line, to the finish line, to be able to say, "I am an Author."

Notes

CHAPTER EIGHTEEN

Prince, Joseph. Health and Wholeness Through the Holy Communion, Fourth edition, Thirtieth print: April 2014. Joseph Prince Resources. https://www.josephprince.com

CHAPTER 23

Nick Vujicic
Australian Christian Evangelist and Motivational Speaker
https://www.Lifewithoutlimbs.org

Dekker, Ted. A.D.30, October 28th, 2014. Center Street.

About the Author

Grace was born into a large family in the north east of England, in the United Kingdom. She is your everyday down to earth Daughter, Sister, Mother, Nanna, Neighbour and Best Friend, intimate in each relationship with a heart of compassion to love, serve, encourage, and help everyone to find freedom and peace to be who they are really meant to be.

Equipped and trained through general life experience of many traumas, dramas and breakthroughs, and many years laid aside through sickness and gleaning on the Word of God, Grace is an avid listener and sounding board in all circumstances. As she responds with sensitivity, godly wisdom, practical application and truth, hope and comfort is released into all areas of brokenness.

Her heart is to love people, meet them where they are at, see them transition as they grasp new truths and apply them to their lives, and have their 'epiphany' moment of transformation change, that brings them into freedom from their physical, emotional and circumstantial bondage. A great encourager and wanting to lead by example, she aims to inspire and empower people to grow, and overcome, as they go through their adversity moments.

Grace used to be quintessentially British: a stiff upper lipped, shy, pretend everything is okay, 'just get on with it', tea drinking, fish and chip loving, family orientated, home loving woman, who stammered, lacked confidence and would do everything to hide in a crowd!

Now, as an overcomer in Jesus, she is healed, free to confront in truth, warm hearted, and life claiming, zealous to share the truth of her experiences through the Word of God, in the power of God, for the glory of God, wherever, and however, she has the opportunity to do so, around the world.

Today, passionate for Jesus with an evangelistic heart, as an author, international speaker, faith coach and mentor, her truth and wisdom in Jesus reaches further afield than the four walls of her living room.

Grace lives in the south east of England, and is the proud mother of three adult children and their respective spouses, and 'Nanna' to four beautiful grandchildren.

Keeping in Touch

If you have made a decision to include God in your life and would like further help and encouragement in your journey, or, if you have a testimony you would like to share after reading this book, please send an email to:

gracertr17@gmail.com

If you would like to invite Grace to speak at your Small Group, Weekend Retreat, Conference, or any other event, please email:

gracertr17@gmail.com

If you would like to view all images in full color, please visit my website at:

www.gracereconciliationministries.com